Praise for *F*ck the Bucket List for the Adventurer*

"In today's world where we seem to have the answers to everything at our fingertips, trekking into the unknown reminds us to question everything. Because we are the only ones who hold our answers. Ayelet Baron guides you as you learn to say yes to life and experience it as never before."

> –Tim McDonald, speaker, guide and former Community Director at *The Huffington Post*

"*F*ck the Bucket List for the Adventurer* is a monumental read, that rare book which speaks to your deepest self. For anyone beginning to challenge the path they've been on, this book is a blueprint for changing your life, an excursion into wisdom and awareness that gets richer with each step."

> – Lynnda Pollio, Multi-award winning Author. Amazon Bestseller in Inspirational Fiction, *Trusting the Currents*.

"This book dispels common myths of what holds us back in our growth and dispenses practical wisdom for anyone on a personal development journey and who is asking the deeper questions. Ayelet cuts through the noise and helps the reader find the necessary focus to make peace with the past in order to truly stand in the present."

> –Rick Snyder, CEO, Invisible Edge and author, *Decisive Intuition*

"*F*ck the Bucket List for the Adventurer: Trekking into the Unknown* is a primer for the courageous heart on the journey to true self-discovery. Ayelet does not do the work for you in this process of divine discovery but she points the way across the threshold. As she says, the way forward involves action and commitment to a goal which might seem hazy but she is there as a companion to accompany you on perhaps the greatest adventure of your lifetime. The journey to YOU!"

> –Flicka Rahn, musician, author, sound healer and educator

"Ayelet Baron speaks directly to that still, small voice in your head whispering that your life could be healthier and more meaningful. Read this book and step into the adventure that is your life."

> Anne Janzer, author of *The Writer's Process*

F*CK THE BUCKET LIST

FOR THE ADVENTURER

Trekking into the Unkown

Book 2

THE UNIVERSE WITH
AYELET BARON

Visit ayeletbaron.com for more information.
Published by Heartpickings
Editing, Design, and Distribution by Bublish, Inc.

Hardback ISBN: 978-1-64704-248-6
Paperback ISBN: 978-1-64704-247-9
eBook ISBN: 978-1-64704-249-3

DEDICATION

This book is for you if ...

You're not stuck in someone else's story
You're a free spirit
You're a curious and courageous adventurer
ready to trek into the unknown

You're ready to start questioning everything, and to
simply say fuck it—or whatever words you choose to
use, when something in life no longer serves you.

OUR ITINERARY

TABLE OF CONTENTS

To be continued . . .

F*ck the Bucket List for the Health-Conscious: Trusting Your Heart

WELCOME BACK TO THE SECOND LEG OF OUR JOURNEY!

"We are all inventors, each sailing out on a voyage of discovery,
guided each by a private chart, of which there is no duplicate.
The world is all gates—all opportunities—
strings of tension waiting to be struck."

— Ralph Waldo Emerson

THERE IS ANOTHER PATH

INTRODUCTION

INTRODUCTION

The wind is a powerful force of nature that we cannot actually see—but we can experience it in other ways. We only become aware of the wind when we hear the trees swaying against it, or see waves rippling in the ocean, or feel a breeze caress our faces. The wind reminds us not to deny or ignore the natural human impulse to explore the unknown with curiosity. The wind, like our breath, reminds us that we're alive.

Imagine, for a moment, that you're a magnificent apple tree. You have deep roots that are constantly seeking minerals and water to keep you alive. You're deeply connected to the Earth and trust in its guidance as you connect and communicate with other trees, fungi, and plants underground. Some of your roots break away and follow an unknown path as you continue to nourish yourself—and in that one act of expanding, you find yourself choosing a different

1

direction. Your roots battle through some extremely hard soil and break through to survive.

The people who walk by on the sidewalk notice that your roots have created cracks in the concrete. They talk about cutting you down, ridding the sidewalk of the messy tree that doesn't understand its place. A debate begins on what to do with you, and your life depends on their decision. Some see you as a hazard and want to take you down for disturbing their pathway. But there's Ruth, a wise woman who sees you and reminds everyone that you provide delicious fruit and much needed shade. "In our every deliberation, we must consider the impact of our decisions on the next seven generations," she says. "Maybe it is we who need to become aware of the cracks in the sidewalk and adapt accordingly?"

When we live in a concrete jungle, nature feels separate and becomes a place where we schedule walks or time to breathe. But when we realize that we're always living as part of nature, there is no separation. We have the opportunity to go within ourselves through healthy practices that help us reflect deeply on who we are. In nature, time stands still, as there is only the light of the day and the darkness of the night to become familiar with.

It is easy to meditate in a quiet room or on a mountaintop, but can you meditate in a crowded space? Jiddu Krishnamurti, a twentieth-century philosopher, helps us see that, "One is never afraid of the unknown; one is afraid of the known coming to an end. The more you know yourself, the more clarity there is. Self-knowledge has no end—you don't come to an achievement; you don't come to a conclusion. It is an endless river. You must understand the whole of life, not just one little part of it. That is why you must read, that is why you must look at the skies, that is why you must sing and dance and write poems and suffer and understand, for all that is life."

LIVING OUT LOUD

This isn't just another self-help book, spiritual book, or memoir—it's an experience, beyond categories and labels, that asks each of us to tap into the universal wisdom that says we can live our lives our own way. I'd like to share upfront that this book is not for everyone. It's for those of us ready to start questioning everything, and to simply say *fuck it*—or whatever words you choose to use—when something in life no longer serves you. This book will help you become more aware of the choices you make. It will help you come to truly know yourself and understand your purpose as a living, breathing, healthy creator of your life. We were born to color with vivid imaginations and live like never before in unity—not conformity or uniformity. Are you ready to discover the wonder of you (Book 1, for the Soul), trek into the unknown (Book 2, for the Adventurer), and trust your heart (Book 3, for the Health Conscious)?

The *F*ck the Bucket* List book trilogy has been created not to dictate meaning, but to inspire you to ask questions, dig deep, and create *your own* meaning. The story starts and ends at your own pace. Once you connect with your own rhythm, you can go on an adventure of a lifetime. These books, like a journey, are a collaboration with the expansiveness of the universe. There are many expeditions we will explore together when we step into the unknown. These expeditions will encourage you to acknowledge the invisible bars that may be holding you captive, allowing you to free yourself from some of the most constricting barriers you've built. These barriers aren't made from material like steel, but rather are infections of the mind, such as believing fear-based stories that jail you in an invisible prison of misbelief.

This book will guide you toward accepting that there is always a way to live a life of meaning. It's up to each of us to become aware of this, accept it, and weave our lessons into an integrated web of life. No one can do this work for you; it's your job to become fully aware that everything's here to be discovered when you let your kindness, beauty, truth, and power shine through with your abundant natural light.

You stand at a juncture of possibilities. Are you entertaining thoughts about a healthier direction in your life? Are you ready to experiment and try things on to see what actually fits you? By doing so, you're opening yourself up to opportunities that were not available until you acted on them. Every action you take, and every thought that precedes it, ushers you into a connection of probabilities and experiences that were not available before. It's up to you to take the action necessary to better understand what's healthy and toxic for your wellbeing. By just taking a few small steps, you can (and will!) get closer to understanding who you are and why you're here. You have within you every capacity to create. Imagine a life where you have nothing to prove to anyone but yourself. Imagine what might happen if you decided to adopt the bold mindset of an adventurer and trek into the unknown. The possibilities are endless.

Are you prepared to take some brave and adventurous steps toward changing restrictions in your life and opening up to a broader range of imagination and transformation? If so, you might discover the universe encouraging you to address your own darkness and guiding you to step into your own light. In doing so, you will find yourself clearing away parts of your life that have caused you pain and hardship. You very well may experience some mind-boggling breakthroughs or mystical moments as you reach deeper into the wisdom and abundance of your soul.

Isn't it interesting that we have constructed our current healthcare system to mainly focus on our physical bodies and assess whether they're ill or healthy? Much of the medical community addresses depression, burnout, Post Traumatic Stress Disorder (PTSD), and other mental health issues, as well as a host of physical issues, with chemicals or psychiatric solutions. This is, of course, because there's more money to be made by dispensing medication to people suffering from a host of diseases. But what if there was a natural alternative to holistically healing ourselves?

Physicists like Nikola Tesla, Albert Einstein and Max Planck introduced the quantum world, which we cannot physically see, filled with vibrations and frequencies. Planck invited us to become aware of the connectedness of our universe when he said, "Science cannot solve the ultimate mystery of nature. And that is because, in the last analysis, we ourselves are a part of the mystery that we are trying to solve."

We accept, in faith, a whole world that is invisible through smart devices, microwaves, radio and television waves, and now, the Internet. What if we started accepting what is in our hearts and let our intuition and deep knowing serve as our internal compass? Our bodies need a balance of the physical and the spiritual to live in harmony. Without this, life falls out of whack with our soul, and we lose our connection to both the visible and invisible worlds around us.

Trekking into the unknown is not just a physical journey—it's about getting in touch with your courage and humility and discovering what has been hidden or suppressed within you. This means exploring both your light and dark sides. It means addressing some of your biggest fears, wounds, and subconscious programming—as well as your unrealized potential. Trekking into the unknown means embarking upon a journey of seeing the weaknesses and the gifts that you've been hiding deep within yourself, out of fear of criticism or rejection.

One of the reasons I've dedicated my life to sharing these universal messages is that I wish I'd had books to tap into when I got lost on my path of trekking into the unknown—simply to let me know that I wasn't alone and I wasn't going crazy. I read, talked to a lot of people, and forged unlikely partnerships, but what I found still left me mostly depleted. This trek often took me down rabbit holes searching for answers, or somebody to guide my journey, only to find people trying to convince me they knew everything when they didn't. I had a hard time when they told me they knew how I felt or that they had been in my shoes. They may have believed they knew what I needed, but in the end, they didn't have a clue. They were not me, and I was not them. And we were all doing our best.

I am a voracious learner and when I recognized that they were making shit up or were too focused on "saving" the world, I simply took the action to walk away. They would talk about the vast importance of love, yet they struggled to express it, and clearly had their own traumas to deal with, like everyone else walking the earth. With some, I experienced firsthand the challenging relationships they had with their own children, and the pain that surrounded their own inability to access the love they talked and preached about. I listened intently, but too often, their actions didn't match what they were saying. This helped me learn to identify who was toxic and who was healthy for my wellbeing. This helped me move away from the hero, victim, and villain stories of our time so I could experiment with what was possible for *me*.

I didn't want to fight for my life anymore in a world designed for division, suffering, and just survival. I wanted peace and a renewed sense of sanity in a world where I felt I was simply going crazy. There was no one to talk to openly about what I was going through, and I lost many friendships and relationships along the journey in pursuit of living life my way. I realized that some people had never been healthy for me, though I had once thought they were. But the people who matter deeply to me are still here. Every day is another opportunity to learn as I step into my own uncharted waters without a manual, referring only to my internal compass and the currents to guide me to live out loud in my own way.

My own journey has raised many questions, and I've gained wisdom from questioning the different expeditions I've experienced. This is what inspires me to encourage you to venture beyond your perceived safety or comfort zone and understand the invisible bars that may be holding you back—and the doors and windows that are waiting to swing open when you're ready to acknowledge them and live out loud in your own way. No longer needing to mask who you truly are.

Every single one of us experiences challenge, trauma, and heartbreak. No one is spared the opportunity to fully experience life. But how we choose to respond is personal. As we wonder, imagine, and expand our hearts and minds beyond what we can physically see and perceive, we'll be able to access more information from within ourselves and our natural surroundings. There is a flow to life, and one of our biggest opportunities is to be curious enough to explore the unknown.

We were born into a natural world where the earth, air, space, water, and fire harmoniously play with each other. Beyond our physical environment, humankind created manmade systems like the military, the government, education, business, and many more that we've been taught to adapt and conform to. Is it really so insane to believe that we could live in a world without war and conflict? Or in a world with an alternative means of education or healthcare?

This is one of the biggest challenges we each face today: resisting the societal conditioning that tells you that you must accept and save these existing systems that no longer serve the vast majority of humanity. Are you going to continue to believe in the programming our ancestors created when it was based solely off self-preservation and survival? What about thriving? Isn't that more appropriate, now that we have evolved as far as we have? Isn't it time to question everything about your current reality? Isn't it time to find your roots and discover with healthy eyes what programs, beliefs, and systems are hurting you at the core? Isn't it time, most of all, to begin imagining and creating healthy systems that truly support you and lift your spirits with pure joy?

By aligning with nature, you may choose to explore whether the Earth has started a major reset without us. We are each at a point in time of healing and letting go of what no longer serves us. Many of us are already striving to become more aware of the unhealthy aspects of our lives. Identifying those unhealthy aspects can empower you to step into the role you play in creating a healthy, fulfilling life for yourself—where you're *thriving* instead of merely *surviving* according to an obsolete playbook. If you've begun this journey or are looking to start, a great way to begin is by making conscious choices about what you consume.

Trekking into the unknown means facing yourself and what's possible for you as a creator of a healthy life. When you start following the compass of intention, curiosity, and courage, nothing will lead you astray. Are you constantly living in the past and playing the same character or role in someone else's comedy, musical, drama, thriller, mystery, tragedy, or horror show? Like the Earth, are you entering a time of reset? Being curious about the unknown and focusing on your opportunity to create—without the external divisions of old systems and societal programming—allows you to experiment with healthy scenarios for yourself with other adventurers who are willing to question, experiment, and co-create.

SOME WALKS WE TAKE ALONE

Wherever you go, there you are. This saying reflects our tendency to constantly want to be going places, as though escaping to a different location will change our reality. But no matter where we go or what we do, we take ourselves and all our baggage with us. When you feel restless or stressed, it might be helpful to channel your feelings into going inside yourself rather than filling your time with external distractions. Sometimes, you may just need a change of perspective, and that's what many of us are being called to do now. We are relearning how to embrace joy and balance in our lives. This is an opportunity to question whether you're being true to yourself or compromising in some way. This journey asks you not to be afraid to be your true self and express yourself in whatever way feels healthy to you.

True freedom is experienced when you unleash your full potential by going deep into the corners of your mind and freeing it from the known. I hope that these words that were entrusted to me can help you apply practical ways of developing your personal power. The universe is here to give whatever level of push you may need, so you can move in whatever direction you feel called to take.

Life is different for each of us. You are at your own stage of understanding why you're here, and how to use the gifts you've been given. It is the trek of a lifetime, and there is no overnight formula for success. It's personal and fluctuates as you grow and learn how to nurture your body, mind, and soul. Nothing remains stagnant. There's a physical and spiritual evolution that is unfolding when you become fully aware of reality and step into the unknown.

The true human journey is one of love, forgiveness, compassion, imagination, courage, and a deep connection to the intelligence of nature. The Greek philosopher, Plotinus, reminds us, "The stars are like letters that inscribe themselves at every moment in the sky. Everything in the world is full of signs. All events are coordinated. All things depend on each other. Everything breathes together."

Through all of the knowing and unknowing, the visible and invisible, facts and mystery, loss and gain, sanity, and insanity of it all—*you are here.* While you may go to bed dreaming of paradise or wake up from a nightmare where you visited hell, you must always remember that every experience is an opportunity to understand your state of mind. For many of us who are busy living our lives or making a living, trekking into the unknown may mean being *still*—a place we've been unconsciously avoiding because we fear what we might discover.

Being yourself is a gift. When you choose to invest in yourself, you can also begin to transform your mental models by accepting that what seemed to work in the past may not be the healthiest way to engage in the future. You may have been taught not to burn bridges, but life teaches us that some bridges take us nowhere and that it might be more beneficial to abandon them altogether.

All you need to pack on your journey is curiosity and courage. A young person may decide that she wants to leave the big city she grew up in to create a community around a healthy way of living—which is also very ancient. Her dream may be to focus on regenerating the land by tapping into what's truly essential in her life and those she cares for. It may be an extremely foreign choice for her family and friends to understand, and some may call her crazy, but it takes the crazy ones who marvel at the wonder of possibility to trek into the unknown. Our world is calling us to create individual and collective visions, aspirations, and realities that we have within us. We are being guided into the unknown to forge healthy paths, accept each other, respect varying perspectives and, above all else, to care deeply about ourselves, each other, and the planet.

When you accept that no one really knows what is best for you, things will break open and fall apart. Our culture has claimed that success can only be achieved when referring to decaying principles and obsolete ideologies, such as relying on authorities for answers instead of looking inward and asking yourself what *feels healthy for me.*

When you don't comply with the status quo and societal norms, you're often shamed, blamed, and ridiculed. Isn't it interesting that you were most likely taught loyalty to others before yourself? Why have so many of us placed our faith, trust, and loyalty in the hands of politicians, business leaders, brands, influencers, philanthropists, musicians, movie stars, and celebrities? How could anyone, outside of you, possibly know what's best for you? And why do you believe they have your answers? It's healthy to shed limiting beliefs and the toxic people in your life who are holding you back. It's healthy to abandon bridges that go nowhere and clear a path to trek into the unknown. There's no manual where you're headed, because you don't need one to get to where you're going. Curiosity, courage, and the mindset of an adventurer is all you'll need to venture into a journey of a lifetime.

TRUSTING OURSELVES CREATES ALCHEMY AND SYNCHRONICITY

We choose whether or not to consume healthy or unhealthy beliefs, foods, and products, and to excuse hurtful behaviors and allow people to treat us in healthy or unhealthy ways. Our beliefs, and the way we have been conditioned, help us justify these choices, while turning our backs on healthy behaviors, beliefs, and people that can enrich and support us. There are millions of reasons why we can't align our minds with our hearts and continue to do what's deemed "right" and "good" at our own expense. But once we become aware that there is another way, we must take responsibility for how our lives are orchestrated. Being responsible means that we're fully accountable for whatever we create—be it healthy or unhealthy. There will be more revealed about this throughout the book as we explore the power behind being the architects of our own lives.

We have the power to choose to not be what others want us to be, regardless of how angry or disappointed they may become. Society, government, friends, and family seem to have a clear idea of how we should live our lives, but that doesn't mean we must yield to that idea. When we choose a path, we learn whether it's healthy or unhealthy for us, and continuously make course corrections and upgrades. When we continuously reach into the past and take the same paths we've always taken, we stay stuck in our rut and can only see the shadows reflecting in our caves. Life is for the living, and while there's sadness, grief, and heartache, loneliness is a choice, as we explored in *F*ck the Bucket List for the Soul*. Life can also flow with abundance when we allow ourselves to experience health, joy, and play.

When you believe that you will never be or have enough—whether it's money, food, emotions or something else entirely—you will experience thoughts and actions that stem from a place of lack. Unlike society, which teaches a scarcity-mindset, nature teaches us there's enough for all of us as we experience the warmth of the sun, the radiance of colors, and the intelligence of trees and fungi beneath our very feet. In his book, *Entangled Life: How Fungi Make Our Worlds, Change Our Minds, and Shape Our Futures*, Biologist Merlin Sheldrake states that he was drawn to fungi because they consist of a variety of humble yet astonishingly versatile organisms. By simply doing what they do regularly, such as, "eating rock, making soil, digesting pollutants, nourishing and killing plants, surviving in space, inducing visions, producing food, making medicines, manipulating animal behavior, and influencing the composition of the Earth's atmosphere, fungi are a truly fascinating thing. Fungi's work is transformational—for instance, they turn biomass into soil and recycle dead organic matter back into organic life. They also have a dark side, with poisonous varieties. And yet, they are mostly invisible to us."

What mindset are you bringing with you every day? What baggage are you carrying around? Can you see what's scarce or abundant in your life and the universe? You can look for the demons in the shadows, call out the evil ones, and judge yourself for not being good enough. Or you can become aware of what you're creating and allow yourself to take a step into the unknown. As the architect of your life, you have the power to shift your thought process to better assess what and who is healthy or unhealthy for you. What type of life do you want to create? What world do you want to co-create? Here you now are—aware and curious enough to dare. What do you choose to bring with you on this journey and what will you leave behind?

Albert Einstein reminds us that, "The important thing is not to stop questioning. Curiosity has its own reason for existing. One cannot help but be in awe when he contemplates the mysteries of eternity, of life, of the marvelous structure of reality. It is enough if one tries merely to comprehend a little of this mystery every day. Never lose a holy curiosity."

Are you ready to embrace your adventurous side and take a walk into the unknown?

Enjoy your adventure!

With deep gratitude,

The Universe with Ayelet

EXPEDITION 10

TAKING THE FIRST STEPS

The desert is an amazing place to become self-aware. The desert is sensual in its raw beauty by being completely exposed to its own nakedness—casting its body in the shadows. The reflection of its raw truth is unavoidable in its entirety. The desert showcases its powerful ruggedness as its rocks endure the intense searing heat of the sun. Escaping to the desert to hike under a blazing sun is a test of self-endurance and strength to persevere through tough times. Only then can we really appreciate a tree that provides protection from the heat, as well as a place to rest and reflect as we hydrate our bodies with clean water. Finding a spot to take a break from the glare of the sun is often necessary to take it all in. To be able to step back and view ourselves as a tiny speck in the universe can transform our experiences into a mysterious and exciting laboratory of opportunity. In *The Gunslinger*, Stephen King wrote, "Any thoughts of guilt, any feelings of regret, had faded. The desert had baked them out."

In the daytime, the desert's intense sunlight feeds us with unbearable heat, while the often-freezing nighttime temperatures are some of the coldest in the world. Every one of us has had to face a tough situation and overcome challenge. Deep reflection helps us understand and appreciate life, and how precious it is. It allows us to cherish the opportunity of life in front of us, because when we step out of the daily insanity of the world, we can stop and face what is truly going by releasing ourselves from the mental prison of fear.

Trekking into the desert and facing the barren, challenging climate can be conducive to developing self-awareness. Staying alert and being self-conscious enough to survive in a hostile environment can give us the confidence to know that we have the tools and awareness to truly see ourselves in meaningful ways. Imagine being in the expansive openness of the desert, looking at its sands. What do you see and experience? A woman gazes at the sand and sees the billions of people in the world who were raised alike, although this world hasn't always been fair towards everyone. The expansiveness of the desert encourages her to pause and realize how precious life is. As she sees the sun rising on the horizon, her soul fills with joy and she gets closer to the reason she was born.

THE WISDOM OF STEPPING INTO THE UNKNOWN

The fear of unknown consequences keeps us rooted in old patterns of the past. Many of us have understood stability through the consistency of our living situations, relationships, paychecks, or the familiarity of nationalities and sports teams. We're now being asked to become healthier, more courageous, resilient, and stronger. Isn't it time to reconsider the meaning of stability, comfort, and safety, and develop a healthy foundation?

Many of us don't like change. We fear change because it's the road to the unknown. The unknown is perceived as dangerous and scary. It's a scientific fact that stress and fear lower our immune systems and make us more susceptible to sickness and disease. We've been conditioned to believe that we must get through our life and, in doing so, we can live happily ever after—without change or transformation. But change is a normal part of life. Change is necessary. Yet, some of us block our natural ability to change in pursuit of survival. And because of so much resistance to change in the world, which stems from us, the pain and suffering we've been conditioned to forces us to *hang on* to what we know when our true opportunities rest on the other side of *letting go.*

But what if the unknown wasn't so scary? How would we know unless we tried experiencing life to the fullest extent? We can't live our lives through other people's experiences and limiting beliefs. What if the unknown is a desert of opportunities, an adventure simply waiting for us? What if life itself is our greatest adventure to be experienced?

Our mindset matters, and when we have the mindset of an opportunity-creator—which we discussed in the first book of this series, *F*ck the Bucket List for the Soul*—the unknown becomes a sea of possibilities where we can rebirth ourselves, our lives, and the world. As Deepak Chopra, author and alternative-medicine advocate, reminds us, "Without uncertainty and the unknown, life is just a stale repetition of outworn memories. You become the victim of the past, and your tormentor today is yourself leftover from yesterday. Relinquish your attachment to the known, step into the unknown, and you will step into the field of all possibilities."

AYELET BARON

NAVIGATING THROUGH TWO WORLDS

Once systems—like business, government, taxation, or marriage—are in place, they defend themselves. The decaying paradigm of the world we created—which is crumbling and hanging on for dear life—is filled with judgment, blame, greed, scarcity, competition, division, violence, loneliness, a need to be right and win at all costs, and the need to mask ourselves into appearing positive and happy, too often at our own expense. This world is mired with problems requiring constant solutions and more innovation in a stress-driven environment that has us consuming toxic beliefs, foods, people and situations. We have created a world we often need to detox and vacate from by fleeing to a tropical island with an iced beverage in our hand, or a silent retreat where we fast for ten days and purge ourselves of the external noise.

We have trusted big-brand food and beverage corporations with our lives by picking up their products from supermarket shelves and bringing them into our homes and bodies. Billions of us have fallen into the trap of believing these corporations are committed to our health and wellbeing, when, in fact, they are only committed to meeting their bottom line, mostly at our own expense. My sister, Anat Baron, in her award-winning documentary film *Beer Wars*, helped us understand the battle for the consumer's wallet through her insider look at the endless challenges craft brewers face against the established large beer giants. The *Los Angeles Times* hit it close to home when it reviewed the film and wrote, "Entrepreneurialism and opportunity go awry when tainted by greed and a thirst for power."

We've all made choices based not on our own research, but on what others are consuming, the way certain foods taste, and how they appear. To this day, many are unaware of the studies showing that sugar is a leading cause of cancer. This information was kept

18

hidden from the public for years. A 2017 article in the journal, *PLOS Biology*, cited internal documents by the Sugar Research Foundation suggesting that knowledge of a possible link between sugar and cancer goes back as far as the 1960s. Even fewer of us are aware that any product we apply to our skin should have zero chemicals. As Magatte Wade, CEO of Skin is Skin, advises, we should be able to eat whatever we put on our skin as it goes into our pores and bloodstream. If you use deodorant, do you know what, if any, chemicals you are putting under your arms? And what about shaving cream, if you use it on your face, legs, or other parts of your body? After doing much research and experimenting, I now rinse my mouth for a few minutes every morning with organic coconut oil and brush my teeth with activated charcoal toothpaste. I keep learning every day how I can be healthier using natural ingredients—something I knew very little about just seven years ago. Many of us were not taught to question the source of the things we consume, or consider who made our latest trendy running shoes, purses, jackets, packaging, and devices, or what they are actually made of.

Conversely, we were taught to *trust* the ingredient lists, and were thus unaware of the need to be on the lookout for hidden additives, chemicals, and growth hormones injected into our food, modifying our children's development. Going to the source makes us aware of who determines how our food is modified and manufactured. But most of us don't know the source of our food, nor do we question the quality of the soil it was grown from, or the chemicals and additives used to enhance feed for animals.

When we go to a store today, the packaging informs us what toxins are not in our food—like genetically modified organisms or antibiotics—instead of telling us what's actually in it. On a trip to the local grocery store, I asked whether a product contained hormones or antibiotics, and was told it was "natural." When I kept asking questions, the two employees behind the counter called in a third who continued telling me it was natural, and I kept asking what that meant. When they couldn't provide an answer, I walked away as they stood around, suddenly aware of why these questions are important for them to ask as well.

Drug companies thrive on our illnesses, including our intolerances to certain foods. There's a pill for everything that offsets what harms us. It's a vicious cycle, as toxic beliefs, food, and people don't come with warning labels. Isn't our real job to monitor our consumption by becoming more aware of what we're introducing to our minds and bodies on a minute-by-minute basis?

If you've ever thought about starting a vegetable garden, you'd first consider whether the soil you've chosen is rich or toxic. You'd then make sure the seeds are free of toxins, as whatever you grow, you will be consuming not just the vegetables but the quality of the soil. Knowing the source is key to everything in life. We all have an opportunity to take impeccable care of our bodies, minds, and souls. We can become conscious of every choice we make. We have forgotten that we're an integrated part of nature and that life is always unfolding and evolving.

When we feel that something is out of balance in our physical system (problem), we can uncover the root cause as opposed to suppressing our symptoms with medication (solution). We only get to the core of the opportunity to heal when we understand the real issue that causes our discomfort, our disease, our dysfunction—and we can take actions and make changes based on that understanding. Everything that is not in harmony suggests that there is something broken within the system, and we can learn to become aware and recognize what is out of balance. Is it the quality of the soil we are planting with? Do we know what is truly healthy or toxic for our immune systems?

This is an opportune time to look at ourselves, our relationships, our environments, our governments, our communities, and all the systems within which we function, and ask, "Are all these systems truly supporting every being that exists in this world?" This is how we can become increasingly aware that the foundation of the paradigms we've created is mostly rotting, and that there is no longer a need to "save *this* way of living in the world" or make this sick world better. It's time for a healthy way forward that doesn't require Band-Aids or fixes. We can activate ourselves to create healthy lives, getting in tune with our own operating systems and building our immune systems by clearing any toxic overgrowth within our own gardens and lands— and by understanding that there's no *them* or *those people*, only *us*.

We can start seeing problems as opportunities and find ways to create bridges to a healthy world that values systems that serve the majority of humanity, not just the one percent—from education, to finances, to law, to healthcare, to community, and anything we can imagine and create. We can decide what material items add value to our lives and what truly brings us joy by focusing on our own healthy lifestyles. The emerging world connects us to the level of reality we are in transition to—integrating life and work with unity, kindness, an opportunity mindset, cooperation, and co-creation. Acknowledging how expansive the human imagination truly is, and recognizing our ability to create newer, healthier systems are so needed right now.

But the current collective fear, greed, divisiveness, conflict, competitiveness, and fear-based thinking knocks us back into decaying paradigms by default. We are being constantly fed unhealthy beliefs and fear so we can consume more and more and more, trying to fill that void. And we're being told one is better than the other when it comes to the economic or political infrastructures we need, for example, but they're all fairly toxic and unhealthy right now—and dividing and fighting over them doesn't serve us. When we adopt an opportunity mindset—which contradicts everything we were raised to believe—we start seeing what has been largely invisible to us. We no longer need to hammer at ourselves day and night to be validated for our success by a broken world.

I met a passionate and driven young man fighting for fairness. I had a father, who I lost half a lifetime ago, who believed in and died from the pursuit of justice. But in a world with corrupt and unjust systems, what's the point of fighting all the time? Why uphold a dying paradigm that doesn't serve the vast majority of us? Why try to save or make this world only "better" when we can take our imagination and courage to create a truly healthy plain of existence? We need imaginative, heart-centered people to trek into the unknown, take the healthy elements of what's working, the insights from what's not working, and create the next wave of economic, political, legal, agricultural, environmental and societal systems that support us.

Ingesting toxic chemicals or beliefs compromises the immune system. It really doesn't take much to support the immune system: eating healthy foods (green, leafy vegetables, and other types of mineral rich vegetables), drinking water as pure as possible, spending time in the sun, and moving our bodies. How can you strengthen your immune system? How can you connect with others and keep your immune system healthy? You can slowly and consciously heal the wounds, the traumas, the energies, and the emotions compromising your immune system—you don't need to relive them over and over in your lifetime. You can tap into your creativity and shake up the box you're living in, giving yourself permission to learn to discover healthier ways to live. What if you can become aware that you're simply navigating through two worlds right now, and start building your own bridges to the world that's emerging right now? Were you not born for this time to unleash your true potential?

THE MINDSET OF AN ADVENTURER

In the film, *Raiders of the Lost Ark*, Indiana Jones—who was played by Harrison Ford—is no ordinary archeologist. When we first meet him in 1936, he's deep in the Peruvian jungle, running a booby-trapped gauntlet to capture a solid-gold idol. Indy ends up losing this artifact to his rival—French archeologist, Belloq—who then prepares to kill our adventurer. In the first of many serial-like escapes, he eludes Belloq by hopping onto a plane. We soon learn that Indiana Jones isn't afraid of much, except snakes.

The next time we see Indy, he's a soft-spoken, bespectacled professor. He's then summoned to find the long-lost Ark of the Covenant. To find the Ark, Indy must first secure a medallion kept under the protection of his old friend, Abner Ravenwood, whose daughter, Marion, evidently has a history with Jones. Whatever their personal differences, Indy and Marion become partners in one action-packed adventure after another, ranging from wandering the snake pits of the Well of Souls to surviving the pyrotechnic unearthing of the sacred Ark.

Adventure and experimentation, perhaps not as ardent as what Indiana Jones went through, can be your guideposts, and you would do well to push yourself out of your comfort zones and welcome new adventures. This could mean venturing somewhere new or simply not limiting yourself. This is the time to say "yes" to life and all it offers you—which isn't always easy. The first step is to question everything when you realize no one has your answers. Where might you be overly sensitive, or reacting to old patterns and programming? When you can break that story and stop reacting to unhealthy programming in the same way, you could potentially experience breakthroughs as you burst through an old paradigm into a healthier, more expansive one. Perhaps now is the time to think about what you can do rather than what you can't, and get your ideas out into your world. Not much will happen until you take the first step—and only you can imagine and explore what it looks like.

Whatever your situation, can you consider throwing back the curtains of life and greeting the day with renewed awe and wonder? Can you tap into your own vast imagination and enter an Indiana Jones vortex where anything goes, and the unknown is a thrilling and scary jaunt? Can you observe and heal any irrational fears and limiting beliefs—such as not feeling good enough—and if so, is it possible to consider the bridges necessary to take you into a healthier existence? How many times have you given up on a dream, an idea, an invention, a new home, a new friend, a new adventure, or a new profession because you blocked it before it could even be birthed?

The only thing we know for sure is that one day we will die. Some, like my father, will die too young, and others will live until past one hundred years of age, never having really lived at all. Surviving from one moment to the next is the current status quo. None of us truly know for certain whether there is a heaven or a hell in the cosmos, but we do know that we can create heaven or hell throughout our lifetime—and some of us have been born into hellish situations and environments from day one.

Many of us have cried, screamed, judged, blamed, and pointed fingers of shame. But once we take back our power through pursuing inner work, we can no longer remain victims. We can no longer afford to hide. The only path we can take is forward, accepting that we have the power to guide ourselves by following our hearts, which beat in harmony with the universe.

We can choose not to allow those with too much wind to blow down our dreams with their negativity or fear. We can hold on through our choices of who and what we consume and stay balanced in what we know to be our divine truth. One way to transform is to start building connections, tunnels, and bridges that make the old ones obsolete. Is there a mysterious and exciting source of inspiration that sparks your sense of wonder and helps you imagine your next adventure?

EVERYONE HAS A PAST, BUT DO WE NEED TO DRAG IT WITH US?

We may have developed a belief that being rich means that we're loved, or that having money and power means that we'll be respected unconditionally. When we have not experienced love, we'll look for ways to obtain it through dominating others in the hope they'll love and respect us in return. We may say we're searching for a community, but it will continue to elude us when all we know is to win at all costs.

When we don't know how to be a team player and are societally programmed to only strive to be the best, this will be our playbook of life experiences. We'll unconsciously attract people to dominate or be dominated by until we can feel safe and comfortable being an equal and valuable player to the team in our own right. Sadly, forever wanting more—more money, more power, more fame, and other conditioned behaviors—is rampant in our current society. These desires ultimately destroy lives, friendships, partnerships, organizations, and our environment.

When you ask anyone whether they faced hardship or trauma in their life, everyone has a story. Fatal illnesses, death, suicide, hurricanes, tornados, pandemics, alcohol, drugs, addictions, depression, earthquakes, fires, floods, car accidents, bankruptcies, poverty, wars, genocide, domestic violence, betrayal, bullying, breakups, sexual abuse, human trafficking—we've all experienced something horrific—often beyond words—that jarred us to the core. Many people have undergone tragic experiences, and often believe they're alone in those events. Every person alive has faced an event that made him or her feel like an anomaly. Hardships are built into the fabric of life and are meant to remind us that we are *alive*.

When these events happen, they often make us believe that we're insufficient and unworthy. "I'm not enough" may start ringing in our minds. It becomes a default mechanism, and we can get stuck in this mindset, allowing it to become the theme for our lives—which is totally understandable, because without being able to talk about our traumas openly, they begin to fester and manifest as shame.

Shame can be devastating for the soul, because it's trying to mask vulnerability and an inability to cope. It perpetuates and feeds the feelings of not being worthy. When such thoughts and beliefs become rooted in our minds as a core belief, we'll find a way to sabotage opportunities when things start going well. Thoughts like, "I'm not smart enough," may pop into our heads.

The mind has the capacity to convince itself—to believe—that the next tornado or disaster is just around the corner. For some people, it also creates a need to prove something to other people—especially those who bullied us or made us feel inferior at some point in our lives. Many have and will spend their entire lives considering *What If* scenarios, only to later understand that they may be doing it at their own expense.

LETTING GO IS A MUSCLE WE CAN DEVELOP

Most of us have been encouraged to be a good person to others— and yet, similarly, most of us have never been encouraged to be kind, gentle, and compassionate with *ourselves* in a pure and loving way. We're now faced with an opportunity to shift our stories, and shed the lifelong practices handed down to us by society and our ancestors. We have an opportunity to become increasingly aware of what drives someone and how that truly impacts us. "One must shed the bad taste of wanting to agree with many. 'Good' is no longer good when one's neighbor mouths it. And how should there be a 'common good'! The term contradicts itself: whatever can be common always has little value. In the end it must be as it is and always has been great things remain for the great, abysses for the profound, nuances and shudders for the refined, and, in brief, all that is rare for the rare," writes Friedrich Nietzsche in *Beyond Good and Evil.*

When I had a successful corporate life in Silicon Valley, I had an insane travel schedule that I became unconsciously addicted to. As a result of flying 300,000 miles a year and constantly crossing international time zones, my body paid the price. I found myself at my local doctor's office in a suburb of San Francisco wearing a white gown, which meant I was already being seen as a patient of a medical establishment. The young doctor came into the examination room hurried and stressed herself. She asked some questions and did some diagnostics. Then, handed me a prescription for meds that she believed would help me. I actually felt worse leaving her office, realizing she spends her day seeing local women, unlike me, handing out prescriptions to lessen and mask our pain and hurt.

She had no idea about my life and had been trained to issue a diagnosis and prescribe a corresponding medication. I threw the prescription in the trash and felt more alone than ever in a world trying to medicate me like everyone else. To not be a victim of the system, I had to question everything so I could learn to take care of my whole self, and understood the doctor was doing her best. It was up to me to find ways to get back in tune with my body by investigating the root cause of what was making me ill. These were all symptoms that my work life was out of balance with real life, and my body was communicating to me that I had crossed some dangerous lines. It was up to me to listen and address the root cause, not medicate or numb myself.

Despite all the success stories we hear, more people are becoming aware that everyone has a story. We can either succumb to be a victim or we can understand that we can control how we choose to respond and show up in our lives. What matters is what action we take with this knowledge. Do we remain stuck in our pasts, or release ourselves by choosing a different path that may be unknown but healthier for us?

WHERE ARE WE GOING?

There was once a caterpillar named Green who felt there was more to life than munching on leaves. One day, he decided to leave the comfort of his home to explore what he was missing out in the world. His search brought him to a very tall pile of caterpillars. Being curious, he decided to join them and try climbing the hill of caterpillars. He had always heard that rules exist for a reason. When you follow them, you succeed; if you don't, your whole world will collapse.

At first, he climbed on top of one, and then another, and soon he was stepping on many others to get higher up in the stack. Green was very competitive, and he was set to reach his goal of being at the top. The more ambitious he became, the more he wanted to win this race. Halfway up, Green locked eyes with another caterpillar, Yellow. They exchanged looks and talked for a minute. But to take the next step, he had to climb up on top of Yellow.

Now that Green had seen her, he found he couldn't step over her. He had no alternative, so they both turned around and made their way down to the bottom of the pile and chose to be together. Green and Yellow created a fulfilling life, until one day his curiosity came back. Green felt that he had to try again and find out what was at the top of the pile. Yellow was sad and tried to talk him out of going to uncover the secret, but Green left anyway.

Green went back to the pile and started climbing again. At the same time, Yellow went for a walk and met another caterpillar, Red, hanging on a branch. Red invited her to join him and transform into a butterfly. She wasn't sure she could because she wanted to be home in case Green returned. But when he didn't come back, she decided to trek into the unknown and join Red.

As Green was getting close to the top of the pile, he suddenly heard screams as some of the caterpillars fell to their deaths. But he wasn't deterred; nothing was going to stop him this time. He carried on. As he got closer to the top, he overheard two caterpillars arguing about not letting anyone know there was really nothing at the top of the pile. There was nothing to achieve by getting to the pinnacle. There was no destination. It was simply a story.

Yellow, however, discovered that there was more to life than eating leaves by trekking into uncharted waters and facing her own courageous transformation. And her exploration ended up changing all their lives.

The metaphor for this story is beautifully illustrated in the book, *Hope for the Flowers*, by Trina Paulus, which addresses the unnecessary suffering incurred clawing our way to the top of the ladder to get ahead in the hope of having a better life. Many of us have been taught to be the caterpillar who yearns to get to the top. It takes time, and sometimes a *lifetime*, to get the clarity we need to find the path that is healthy for us. It's like being trapped in a maze where we are too focused on the destination rather than the journey. We often become so busy achieving, arriving, and winning that we cannot see clearly, and everything becomes an anxious whirl causing ourselves more and more harm.

WHEN SYSTEMS NEED A REBOOT

We mostly rely on metrics that respond to an old system, but what if these indicators cannot predict anything from here on? What if what we're facing right now, as we trek into the unknown, is an opportunity to become aware of the stagnant systems that no longer serve us? What if we no longer want to climb to the top? When a system is broken, it will cease to function. Processes that are broken will not reboot easily.

When we feel a sense of despair and need help with the systemic issues of our mind, we might reach out to a therapist, a mental health expert, a psychiatrist, or a psychologist. We may feel trapped and overwhelmed by life, unable see a way out of the dark tunnel we find ourselves in. A wise guide will recommend taking a breath and quieting the mind of fearful thoughts. He or she will suggest forgetting about expectations and letting go of the impulse to fit into the sameness society conditions us to value. A healthy guide will encourage us to find a way to go to a neutral zero point that will allow us to pause for whatever length of time is necessary to recalibrate. It's a process where we let our intuitions flow without all the busyness of life, which is stressful.

Surround yourself with trees. Observe the sunrise and the sunset. Watch and listen to birds. Spend time with horses and goats. Observe a crow chase an eagle. They will show you what's always been here. Can you take a conscious breath and go deep inside yourself to understand what resonates with you, and what doesn't anymore?

Take a hard look around you. Author Shannon L. Alder wrote, "People that hold onto hate for so long do so because they want to avoid dealing with their pain. They falsely believe if they forgive, they are letting their enemy believe they are a doormat. What they don't understand is hatred can't be isolated or turned off. It manifests in their health, choices, and belief systems. Their values and religious beliefs make adjustments to justify their negative emotions. Not unlike malware infesting a hard drive, their spirit slowly becomes corrupted and they make choices that don't make logical sense to others. Hatred left unaddressed will crash a person's spirit. The only thing he or she can do is to reboot, by fixing him or herself, not others. This might require installing a firewall of boundaries or parental controls on their emotions. Regardless of the approach, we are all connected on this 'network of life' and each of us is responsible for cleaning up our spiritual registry." And what happens when that hate and anger is also pointed at ourselves?

A reboot lets us release what's broken, so those stagnant systemic issues are no longer there when we rebound. Humans are incredibly resilient beings; we're always able to start over and begin again. When we become aware of what no longer serves us, we can see the opportunities instead of just the problems, discovering the courage to face the unknown with curiosity. Systems that were not working, processes that were almost broken, don't need to be rebooted, just like us.

Each of us can examine our unconscious wounds and programs that have been instilled in us since childhood and throughout our adolescence by parents, ancestors, authority figures, or these very systems. We can carry our trauma with us or get the help we need to neutralize it. Those introducing zero-point practices advise us to start by identifying the unconscious individual and collective programs that run deep inside of us, so we can consciously let them go.

When we consciously go down to zero and start coming back, the dysfunctional attributes no longer need to drain us. Can you see how this works? When you're at zero, you come back different. There's no need to accept what's unhealthy for you and get back to the old programming. It's up to you to discover what works for you and start investing in what matters, by laying the foundation for a life that is anchored in healthy, nature-based opportunities.

AN UNKNOWN VERSION OF NEUTRALITY (ZERO-POINT)

How many of us have mastered reaching a calm state in the midst of a struggle, conflict, trauma, or transition? When a sense of balance is achieved, higher levels of information, awareness, and support become more readily accessible. It's easier said than done, however, which is why we should experiment attaining a state of neutrality in our own way. Neutrality doesn't mean that we don't care or feel deeply. Practicing neutrality allows us to step out of a story or situation and become the observer of our experience through a different perspective. It allows us to pause, and see a cycle or pattern in our lives, so we can understand it and forgive ourselves or each other. It allows us to expand with new information and flow beyond our limited perspective so we can get fully in touch with ourselves.

Imagine a recent stressful situation you've experienced. Did you feel angry, sad, disappointed, hurt, or deeply betrayed? How did you react? Did you throw an item across the room, yell at the top of your lungs, cry, or express your hurt to someone else, replaying the injustice you experienced? All of this is very real—it's how you felt at the moment. Do you know what your response pattern tends to be? The first step for me was to become aware of how I was hardwired to respond to stressful situations. This was when I realized I would often spend time rehashing my negative experiences with a friend.

I started to understand that it wasn't about how life was treating me, but how I was treating life that mattered. In his life-changing book, *Man's Search for Meaning*, Viktor E. Frankl shared, "It did not really matter what we expected from life, but rather what life expected from us. We needed to stop asking about the meaning of life, and instead to think of ourselves as those who were being questioned by life—daily and hourly. Life ultimately means taking the responsibility to find the answer to its problems and to fulfill the tasks which it constantly sets for each individual."

A few years ago, a friend introduced me to a different type of neutrality—one we can each access. She explained that there's another neutrality, which is referred to as "zero point," or holistic, full-spectrum grounding. Any time I focused my energy on a problem or something I resisted; I was actually expanding it. The best way for me to explain the pattern I saw around how I responded is relating it to bodysurfing in the ocean. When a big wave would come in behind me, I could jump and meet it and let it roll over me. When I fought the wave, it would hurt like hell and I could feel a burn throughout my body. When I was neutral and aware of the wave coming toward me, the wave would lift me, and I felt like I was floating on air with no resistance. It didn't mean I was indifferent, but that I was aware of my ability to trust the currents.

We need a lot of patience when our reality becomes very demanding. But what if it demands that we persevere in the neutral gear, so we can be grounded, held steady, and remain firmly connected to the Earth? Enduring through all the twists and turns, we can develop a relationship with our mind to trust and let life unfold. This is true, whether we're orchestrating harmony in our professional lives or our personal ones.

Connecting with the inner self promotes true harmony. We're tested and challenged at different times in our life so we can adjust and transform. We unlearn only to relearn things differently. We reinvent in order to rebuild ourselves. We've been wired with an enthusiasm to explore and to question—and, along the way, we can discover our capacity for compassion and self-love.

This is where part of the issue lies. So many of us become totally focused on the goal, the destination, or the list of everything we must achieve. We become so busy climbing the ladder of success that we don't remember why we want to be successful in the first place. But we're all taught to aspire to get there, and to add items to our bucket list with the promise that once we do, our lives will be worth living. And we may have that moment of glory, but it, too, is fleeting. Until we walk out into the unknown, the odds of fully experiencing the natural beauty of our lives are pretty low.

BECOMING AWARE OF THE NEED TO RELEASE

You have the option of releasing the harmful, limiting beliefs you've been holding on to, or you have the option of continuing to cling to them. Letting go of what no longer serves you allows you to expand, by shifting your focus toward the opportunities in front of you, instead of the problems. It allows you to turn off the news that may bring you stress, worry, or fear, and instead spend that time getting grounded in possibility. Would you continually eat toxic food if you knew it causes cancer? Would you make different choices if you knew the source of a product was harmful to the health of children? Would you buy products from or work for a company that treated its employees no better than instruments of slave labor? Would you continue to consume beliefs and news that cause you stress and anxiety?

When you're stuck in playing a part in someone else's story, it's not easy to ask any of these questions, and it's even harder to truthfully answer them. It requires you to take a step back and go to an uncomfortable place with a heavy heart, since you don't want to acknowledge that you may have been duped, or that the world we constructed never served the vast majority of humanity—only the few.

But you didn't come to this planet to suffer or feel depressed or fight for your life. When you realize this and accept that you have the power to define, explore, and discover your own sense of happiness, much can shift within you. You can start by controlling the volume of the noise around you and realize that you actually came here to create and experience joy in many forms. Can you imagine the world you want to live in? What's your role within it? Do you ever go deep and ask yourself, "Why am I here?"

The process of becoming increasingly aware of the fact that there is another way to life—that you don't need to stay trapped in a paradigm that is dying—causes immense shifts. Your thoughts of fear or joy impact the way your body and mind function. Releasing the weight of negative thinking and emotion helps you become lighter and more open to creation, but it takes practice and work.

I met a man who had gone through tremendous hardships throughout his life and carried them with him everywhere he went—in his thoughts, conversations, and beliefs. He would overcome one roadblock only for a new one to emerge shortly after. Len had a brilliant mind and could easily counsel others, but he was unable to free *himself*. He talked about faith and waited for a sign outside of himself for guidance on what to do next with his life—while, at the same time, expecting more doom and gloom to present itself, be it his fear of becoming homeless or running out of money. What he didn't understand was that moving to another town would not change much for him until he took the first step to release his baggage and do the work he came here to do. Because wherever you go, there you are. There's no hall pass being handed out to any of us. No hocus pocus or fairy dust a guru or shaman can sprinkle over us. No one is coming to save us from ourselves.

"The real voyage of discovery consists not in seeking new landscapes but in having new eyes." This sentiment by Marcel

Proust reflects the theme of trekking into the unknown as a curious adventurer. This is a great opportunity to:

- Explore your imagination, ideas or philosophies
- Question everything
- Explore and challenge your belief system
- Become aware of what trekking into the unknown means to you and see whether you're ready, or not, to take the first step. Only you know when you're really ready

So many of us seek a sign or a message, and yet when we see with healthy eyes, the message is within us. We just have to open ourselves to the possibility that when we stop seeking, it may be around us all the time. We can free our minds from the problems of unnecessary restrictions, as healthy thoughts and realizations flood into our awareness. Being present is not the same as accepting things as they are.

Opportunities appear in our lives because we've made the space for them to emerge. This process goes far beyond restructuring our thoughts, emotions, and body. What this actually means is that we start observing ourselves—without judgment, blame, or a need to be right. By virtue of judgement-free self-observation alone, it is easy to realize that being stuck in a winning mentality, or having to always be right, holds no personal benefit. What is the point of being divided and conflicted with ourselves and each other? When you get to the bottom of it, who are the real winners and who are the real losers? And why have we constricted our world in this unnatural way?

Our world needs us to let go of the past stories of caped superheroes and warriors saving us. No one wants to be saved or fixed or changed. What happens when you release your hold on the past? What happens when you are able to see that kindness, compassion, and generosity have been waiting for you to fully embrace them? What boundaries are holding you back? What do you truly need in your life to feel fulfilled? These are all questions that are addressed throughout this book with real-life stories and opportunities to discover your own questions and answers.

FORGIVENESS IS ANOTHER MUSCLE TO ACTIVATE

Forgiveness is surfacing in scientific research as an important element in health and wellbeing. The healing power of forgiveness can decrease physical pain and stress, strengthen our immune systems, decrease the risk of a heart attack, and greatly strengthen relationships. When we begin to forgive ourselves, our heart opens to forgive others. Forgiveness starts with each of us, and to be human is to err—to be vulnerable, authentic, and real. The question is, are you ready to look at where *you* may be stuck? Are you ready to shine a light on what really is going on for you? Can you look objectively at where you have been, so you can become aware of where you truly want to go?

None of this will happen until you're ready to truly see with your own eyes and feel with your own heart. Being ready is unique to each of us, as it depends on becoming more in touch with ourselves, the opportunities that surround us, and the invisible bars that are jailing us in a mental prison. When we're ready, we'll realize we're *enough*. We'll realize how powerful we are within ourselves. There will be no need to dominate others or nature, and we can slowly find ways to take steps forward at our own pace, with a healthy dose of self-forgiveness and self-awareness. There's no reason to drag our hurt and pain along with us when we can also examine and heal it.

Wrong turns, unexpected decisions, and unhealthy choices have contributed to who and where we are now. The beauty of forgiveness is that we can let go and stop recreating and reenacting the same behavior in our lives. Embracing the past with compassion and forgiveness can help us appreciate what we've gained from each of our experiences, even if the outcomes were disappointing and not what we wanted or expected at the time.

We're not living in a Hollywood movie where the formula for saving the world is a superhero confronting and taking down the evil villain so everyone can live happily ever after. All we achieve by exacting revenge is making ourselves equals of those who have hurt us—whereas, forgiveness practices humility and understanding. To resist revenge and pledge ourselves to forgiveness is to break the cycle of human history and respect our capacity to practice self-care. We can't continue this insane cycle of revenge, as it never ends. And if we choose to, it's the same story over and over and over again—just maybe a different channel. When we spend all our energy focused on what's good or bad about somebody else, we often end up exhausted and defeated by the time we've spent judging others.

What we're not taught in school is how to make peace with ourselves and the world around us, especially when it comes to our past. For peace to be created, forgiveness, acceptance, trust, and gratitude come first. You may discover other qualities or energies that you need, as there's no formula for how to plant your unique seeds. You can trek into the unknown and ask yourself, "What would help me make peace with myself and my past, and what is the first conscious step I'm ready to take?"

EXPEDITION 11

NAVIGATING UNCHARTED TERRITORY

E very person and situation that crosses our path is here to teach us something—and how we react also teaches us something about ourselves. We can learn from every interaction, whether we're ready for the lesson or not. When we surround ourselves with people who are angry, who love to blame others, and who always seem to be victimized, we'll spend much of our life engrossed in their never-ending tales of drama and idle chatter. People get a lot of their energy and recognition from creating drama. It's our choice not to participate in their play, unless we truly feel there is something for us to learn from the experience.

The question to ask ourselves here is whether we're offering assistance at our own expense. There really is no reason to chase someone else's story. Sometimes, we may be so hungry for connection, we'll experiment with different groups, or follow trendsetters or popular social media platforms for answers. Either way, we're taught to find the answers to our personal problems by looking outside of ourselves, and that is the very opposite direction of where we could be heading. This is an easy trap to fall into, however, because it's possible to occasionally find answers from the outside world that feel satisfying for the moment.

It's important to recognize how much time and effort we spend dealing with the stress of our careers and the drama of our relationships. They take up a lot of our energy, and a part of us is always aware of the fact that we don't *have* to be so entangled. Accepting this while knowing and acting upon it is what's challenging. When we accept this, we can change our behavior and better protect our own energy, remaining alert and not falling back into the cycle of creating drama to fill the void of no drama.

Our world can be chaotic, demanding, and complex—or, it can be very simple. There are so many boxes and bars to cross that we don't always know where and how to start. There are many people who hate their jobs or find themselves in toxic relationships, but our fear of the unknown is so great, we prefer to stay in a bad situation just because it's familiar. Some of these fears are unhealthy, and others are made-up stories of why we cannot make healthier choices. When we are increasingly aware of what we truly need in life (our *enough*), we can become more rational about our fears and deal with them head on.

We're so defined today by how we pay our bills and the lifestyle we think we need that we get stuck in a box that feeds many of our most irrational fears. Why not imagine, with a healthy mindset, that there is another way? Another way to take care of your bills when you know what your *enough* is? It might not be perfect, but this path is ready and waiting to be experienced. There are no guarantees, but things could go incredibly well, and you would never know if you didn't try. If there are hurdles and bumps along the way, there is another lesson to experience and another choice to make. Nothing is set in stone unless you're a stone.

Often, when things don't go the way we planned or expected, we spiral in disappointment and heartbreak. No one teaches us that the job that didn't work out, the friendship that broke apart, or the love that was not reciprocated was actually a gift. Why? Because we associate all of these activities with failure—but that is societal conditioning, not reality. Would your mother, for example, rather tell her friends that you're married, even if you're miserable, than admit that you're divorced with little ones? Nobody wants to experience a flat tire while on a road trip. The inconvenience and the delay can be aggravating. But, just think—that delay could very well cause you to avoid a pileup that occurred a few miles further down the road. There is often a blessing in the inconveniences and challenges we experience, even when we can't see them right away.

We are living at a time when many of the concepts we grew up with—like shame and success, for example—are now considered very destructive and desperately need to be reexamined. Isn't it time to learn how to be gentle with ourselves and others? Is it really better going to a job we hate every day, or staying in a loveless relationship, or investing in a friendship that drains us? To feed our souls, empathy for ourselves is needed, or we will end up empty and unavailable to ourselves and others.

TRY DEMANDING YOUR PLANTS TO GROW OVERNIGHT

Jerry Garcia of the Grateful Dead advises us that "Constantly choosing the lesser of two evils is still choosing evil." When we believe there's

AYELET BARON

only one proven route to success, it's almost impossible to imagine anything else. How many times have you heard someone talk about an election and say, "well, this person (insert name) is the lesser of two evils"? How did we get to a place where our choice is to pick between who is less awful to *lead* our countries, our organizations, our lives and our communities? Why do we choose to accept that there's no other path to step out of our collective history and create mechanisms for healthy people who bring unity, not division, to serve as our leaders? Don't we deserve to have a more meaningful way of living than to endlessly bump up against terrible choices? Isn't it time for leadership to be meaningful and have people who truly walk their talk represent us?

It starts with each of us when we trek into the unknown. To step out of this mess, we can start our days with questions and explore what our role is in each situation, not wait for someone else to lead us. Understanding what you expect from the outside world may help you become increasingly aware of the rules and standards you have set for yourself. You can ask yourself whether your beliefs, choices, and decisions are aligned and integrated enough to bring meaning to your own life. It doesn't matter where you are right now in terms of execution. It's far more important to have the clarity of your intentions and question everything.

Inner reflection is an opportunity to get in touch with your authentic voice and intuition, which may have become muffled by the noise of the external world. When you, and only you, can recognize that you can go beyond where you were guided and not accept the status quo, you will no longer evaluate a situation as being "better" or "worse." You will start questioning what's possible and consider what your own unique standards are.

Take a breath and feel what flows through you as you become conscious of your breath. Now, take an inventory all the failures, challenging people, and tough situations that make up your past and jot down what comes through. Ask yourself, "what has complicated my life today because of the baggage I'm holding on to? What difficulties have come into my path that refuse to budge when I push against them?" And by no means, do you need to criticize, rank, or prioritize any of them. Each experience and person brought you here today. The question is which, if any, are still relevant.

Now, take another breath and capture all that you wish to change or abolish, all you admire about yourself, all you desire, all you have yet to attain from your bucket list (if you have one). Ask yourself, "what am I going to do to accept the past and plant the seeds for the future?" You are now in the realm of reconstruction and it's up to you to reclaim your power. It's acceptance of all that you are—all that you have been and all you have yet to become—that allows your truth to materialize. Mastery emerges through trust and faith in the unknown. Only you can tap into your pure essence and ability to explore what's possible.

The tomato seeds you planted in the garden don't grow four or five inches overnight. You can't wake up disappointed and declare that the seeds don't know how to grow anymore. You know they have to be watered and nurtured, otherwise, they will die. They need a foundation of rich soil to thrive. You are no different. You may question your ability to make enough money to survive. You may rush around trying to be fixed—or worse, trying to fix others—in the name of saving the world. There is a never-ending search for the magic and secret sauce, without realizing all you can do is unfold naturally within yourself, with divine timing. Imagine standing in the doorway of a large room next to the light switch. You have the choice to turn the switch on or off. You can choose whether you want to stay in the dark and be enslaved by it or light up the room to explore what's possible.

Be aware of the choices you're making. Consider whether or not you're giving your power away to some external force or authority or ancestral voice playing in your mind of how your life should be. Much of suffering comes from fear and a lack of courage to follow your intuition. Many people have unknowingly constrained ourselves through limiting belief systems. You can spend your life seeking approval or trying to live up to someone else's expectations or set unrealistic goals you believe you must achieve in order to find happiness. The subliminal code of our society is constantly emitting the belief that in order to "be somebody," you must achieve a certain level of societally defined success. What if you stopped and took a look at what it means to be happy *and* successful? The code forgets to tailor itself to individual experiences; its overarching message is meant to be a one-size-fits-all, but that isn't reasonable. The message is generic and implies that all one needs to be happy can be accessed through obtaining wealth. When you are successful, not only will you be able to have whatever money can buy, you will also be socially honored and revered.

We unconsciously place children in an education system with the expectation that they will graduate and earn a good living—which will then bring them happiness and success, just as our societal code implies. When you listen in on a conversation between two parents talking about their children, it wouldn't matter their ages, as the essence of the topic would remain the same—sharing their successes in potty training, learning to walk, reading, writing, graduating high school, earning a degree, landing a good job, getting engaged, living in a great location. The stories continue on and on. We pass down the same belief—the same subliminal, societal code—and expect our successors to follow the same rules that were handed down to us.

What many are starting to realize is that the Money = Success + Happiness formula is false for many of us. It doesn't work this way, because happiness is unique to each of us. Some of the happiest people I've met live in an off-grid tiny house. Success might bring temporary happiness, but that happiness only lasts until we wake up from numbing ourselves with purchasing material items—with which we'll almost certainly become bored, as they no longer gratify our needs.

We can get off course and become addicted to the illusion of power that money brings, or avidly pursue a bigger slice of pie at the expense of others, but if we were ever to see behind closed doors, we'd witness their suffering in the dark, too. The constant need to have more, more, more, and be the best comes at a cost no one tells us about. Some people want to be efficient and productive and win at all costs, while the real opportunity is to learn to flow and create something meaningful for ourselves and others. Nature does not rush, and yet it is raw and real, like time spent hiking in the desert.

DISRUPT YOURSELF FROM THE INSIDE OUT

Most young adults start their careers at a base salary, with the goal to move up the ladder of success so they can earn more money, more prestige, and more benefits. This is how we have been programmed to be rewarded for hard work. So, some move up, and now they're making six figures—and yet, happiness and success are still eluding them. On the other side of the coin, some find success immediately and earn their first million dollars, but the euphoria is only fleeting and the magic they were promised still disappears.

Euphoria comes from *inside* of you and it's up to you to discover what sparks you about the unknown and how you want to experience this life. When you're looking for euphoria from others, it will always be temporary. The more you look inside yourself and listen to how you really want to experience your life, the easier it is to course-correct and begin living authentically. It is this authenticity that will lead you to euphoria again. So when you're ready, take an inventory of what ignites you, what excites you, and what opportunities will help you release the adventurer in you.

Each one of us knows that when we feel resistance, something is off. It's up to us to listen to those feelings. If we choose to ignore them, hoping they will go away, we'll find ourselves going down a rabbit hole. Needing more and more knowledge, love, recognition, power, or money becomes a sort of addiction, and the more we grapple with the dark—and seek help with pills, alcohol, or food—the more we become lost to ourselves, as all we'll succeed in doing is dimming our own light.

I mentored a lot of brilliant young women who had a strong desire to be promoted to the coveted role of Director. I shared with them, from personal experience, to never let anyone know how much they wanted this promotion, as it would only be used against them as a carrot to work harder and harder, without being rewarded for their contributions. And once they finally got there, it would actually lose its meaning.

People are readily available to provide solutions outside ourselves, because our societal code focuses on the quick fix. The route to our own personal happiness and success involves decommissioning and unlearning limiting beliefs instilled deep inside, which we dove into in *F*ck the Bucket List for the Soul: Discover the Wonder of You* in great detail. There are no quick fixes to untangle decades of missteps. The manuals of societal success no longer apply to a vast percentage of the population, and yet, so many continue to hang on in the hopes it will lead to happiness. History shows that it rarely does.

Think about what you do. Now, think about who you are. Are these parts aligned or misaligned? Do these two parts feel integrated and harmonious together? If not, is it time to consider making an adjustment and search for a new part inside you that unites them?

Is it healthier to have experienced and immersed yourself in a full and rich life with setbacks and failures, rather than sit on the sidelines and criticize everything and everyone? Fear is alive and well in the corridors and hallways of our minds. It's a wonderful gift to behold when we know we need to experience failure as well as success. We really can only learn through trial and error and reach a new level of understanding when we have both perspectives and experiences.

Every person has his or her own personal record of failure, and we can empower ourselves more when we're willing to learn and grow from our experiences. Imagine if we were able to openly celebrate our failures. There would be no need to hide or be ashamed of them. Where are you now because of your failures? Are you still suffering and being victimized, or did the knowledge give you self-esteem and confidence to skip the landmine the next time it appeared on your path?

YOU DON'T HAVE TO BE A WORK OF FICTION

We learn from a young age to repair things that are broken—and consequently, we're often taught that we must also fix ourselves, others, and the world. We also downloaded the vibration of unhealthy fear around not being perfect as a living, breathing, pulsing energy that consumes our lives, like the game children play called "telephone," where they whisper a message ear-to-ear, going all the way around a circle of participants. In the end, the original message has become misconstrued into something completely unrecognizable, and everyone either laughs or feels bad about getting it wrong—how we react depends on our internal wiring and conditioning.

But anything broken is rarely the same again and leads you into the unknown, when you choose to start laughing from the depth of your gut. What's whispering to you right now? Is there anything that has you tossing and turning at night? Or is there something that has you so stressed and exhausted that you can barely keep awake? The first step is to become aware of the energy of fear pulsating through your veins and what relationship you want to have with it.

Do you remember the story, The Emperor's New Clothes? It's a tale about human vanity that reminds us of the never-ending human desire for power, influence, material success, fame, and prestige. If the emperor has no clothes, and people are just pretending he's clothed because they're conforming to the crowd, the situation ends when people stop repeating the lie. It's as simple as that.

When we stop doing what we're told—and publicly announce that the emperor is parading through the streets buck naked, for example—we don't need to live in "pretend land" and are free to move on with other aspects of life. We can choose not to be the voice for someone else's message or agenda. There's no need to celebrate the emperor without clothes, pretending he is wearing a magnificent robe. Let people be what they are. But let's become aware of how we truly want to show up in our own lives.

We reveal our true selves through actions, not words, and we often make the mistake of choosing to ignore the signs and not acknowledge that someone is full of shit. We tell ourselves, "He didn't really mean it," or, "She's not like that," or, "I can help her." We're conditioned by this societal code to trust others before we learn how to trust ourselves and our intuitions. This happens a lot professionally. There is an expectation that we must fix a certain situation or resolve disagreements or conflicts. It doesn't matter how many conflict-resolution classes we sit through; we will inevitably fail to find a satisfactory resolution until we start with ourselves.

Within the deepest part of yourself, there exists a core identity that only you can access. You will never truly master communication until you learn to have deeper conversations with all these parts inside of you and learn to integrate them. Most of my own failures happened when I acted prematurely and tried to find a quick fix to a conflict. It was always due to an external pressure to hurry up and find a solution. It was during these times, when I didn't practice what I learned in the jungle about patience and sitting back to reflect.

When we rush in with a solution, we're seeing everything in front of us as a problem, and we're already designing the answer for it. Our true opportunity is to take a deep breath and step out of the situation in order to assess it and find the way forward by understanding the deeper root cause. When we're constantly reacting, we block off our imaginations and put ourselves back in the same cycle.

When we're feeling pressured, we tend to hurry and anxiously come up with a solution. In the rush and anxiety, we'll more than likely lose sight of why we're excited about something. To build solid and trusted relationships with anyone—especially ourselves—takes time. No amount of rushing or pushing will build them quicker. As with the apples, racing to pick them sooner will not bring a better harvest. A relationship founded on trust and respect will yield to more effortless and meaningful collaboration, bringing the most valuable assets together so everyone benefits.

We're somewhat stuck in this transactional mindset that takes us from activity to activity without awareness. So, when an opportunity comes along, we miss it or are taken by surprise and caught off guard that it has to come around again.

What happens when you choose not to take anything for granted and not to let your ego run amok? Circumstances are known to change, as energy is constantly in motion. Sometimes you make the change and sometimes the change catches you. Change is not waiting for you and can appear when you least expect it. Growing up in a war-torn country, I learned from a young age how much can change in a moment. The threat of war or terrorist attack was always in the air, which helped me forge a different relationship with uncertainty and drove my desire for a world with no division, no sides, and no need to fight for our lives.

WE LEARN AS WE GROW AND CHALLENGE OURSELVES

There was a young child I met in Johannesburg when I took a break from a business trip to visit the local community. He grew up in a shanty town of shacks made from corrugated metal, plywood, cardboard boxes, and sheets of plastic. There was no sanitation, water, electricity, or other basic needs provided. This young boy took me into his shack with a big grin, showing me where he lived with his entire family. To him, it was home sweet home. Everyone around him told him how lucky he was to not live on the streets and to have a safe place to live in, and he believed them.

When a small child is led to believe that his environment is perfect and wonderful, why wouldn't he think it was? I stayed in touch with him and, as he got older and experienced more of the world, he started to question his surroundings. Why did his entire family live in one room? Why didn't they have clean water or electricity? Instead of feeling defeated, he started spending his life creating healthier alternatives to living as opposed to accepting this status quo.

Our history can keep us chained in pain and hurt with no roadmap for how to navigate the insanity we may find ourselves in. We can't change how we got here. It serves no one to get stuck in the past, unless we're learning from it. We can't go back and fix it, but we can learn from it and break the cycles. We can also understand when, what happened in the past, should never happen again. Be thankful when you start to really become aware of the ride, you're on and the game you find yourself in. Sometimes, there's no explanation as to why you're going through the trials you are, especially when you find them challenging. The skill you can develop is an ability to navigate your way out of the box you feel stuck in. Situations will appear again and again, until the lesson is learned. Part of the lesson is also becoming fully aware of how you choose to react and respond to situations and people.

You can also become aware of your emotions and how your body is responding. Each time you observe yourself without judgement—your behaviors, reflexes, and reactions—you are better equipped to course-correct and take control of the only thing you can: your response to negative events. Experiences are here to teach you, so embrace them and allow them to take you where you're meant to go. Allow yourself to develop healthy skills along the way to help you move forward and let the past go.

When hiking in the Amazon Rainforest, you keep your hands in your pockets so you don't grab onto anything surprising when you fall—and it's almost guaranteed that at some point, you *will* fall. The local guide clears the path with a machete, as there are no paved roads to where you're headed. As you make your way, your boots may get stuck in the mud, and you may feel like you are quickly sinking into quicksand. It catches you by surprise, and as you feel yourself being swallowed by the earth; you literally freeze, unable to take a step forward. You slowly sense the mud and water sloshing inside your boots as two tribespeople effortlessly lift you out of the mess you got yourself into. While you're covered in protective gear from head to toe, the guides wear very little and move back to the front, swinging their machetes. One stays with you to help you align your pace with that of the jungle, focused more on what's in front of you than dealing with the fear of the unknown in your mind.

When you're ready to explore what is possible, you can take charge and choose a direction that captures your imagination. If you choose to walk backwards or stay stuck in the quicksand, it is almost impossible to navigate. It's healthy to learn from the past so you don't keep repeating mistakes or misadventures. The past is an incredible teacher, enabling us to look back and remember the great lessons to build upon, like the child who woke up to the reality and realization he was not living in a castle. Once he experienced having access to clean water and sanitation, he wanted to have healthier living conditions and change his surroundings. What you learn is that your mindset is so powerful, you can determine and create your own heaven or hell based on how you see the world and the conditions you are in.

Being in shanty towns and slums around the world impacted me deeply. When I returned from my business trips and sat comfortably in our offices in Silicon Valley, London, Singapore, or Toronto, I would bring these experiences with me. It was hard to experience the inequities of the world we created firsthand, and yet I could only be an advocate, helping to introduce healthier practices and spark conversations that enact positive change.

I'll never forget a live video call, using Telepresence technology, between a group of young girls in Africa, Latin America, and Canada. At the beginning, we had to jump in and facilitate the conversation until the girls felt comfortable with each other. They soon found they had a lot in common, despite living in varying circumstances. At one point, one of the girls from Nigeria asked whether all the other girls on the call also lived in one room with their family. There was silence. I was in our Toronto office and felt the discomfort that spread across the room. Most of the girls never had to share a room, let alone have their entire family live in only one room.

What happened next was a meaningful conversation that took the dialogue between the girls to a higher level of connection as they started engaging more deeply. It also showcased the beautiful power of technology that allowed people to connect through open dialogue and share their experiences. Some of the girls later became friends on Snapchat or Facebook and continued to stay in touch, because, at the end, apart from the material aspects, they had more in common than they imagined when it came to insecurities, boys, dreams, and so much more.

WHO HOLDS YOUR POWER?

The quality of love or fear that you bring to each situation determines which path you will take. Even in the darkest moments, you can find hope and love in knowing that you live in a beautiful, significant, and connected universe. All you can do with your past is learn from it. Holding on to it is detrimental and keeps you anchored there. You can seek out professional help when you're dealing with deep scars or trauma. You don't need to go it alone, as there are people who can truly help you. But choose wisely. Make sure they practice what they preach. It takes work to find the people who truly *get* you.

Traveling and meeting people from all over the world, I realized that I did not see loneliness or depression in places where people were simply looking for their next meal. And while I heard so many people tell me that money is the answer—and yes, it is for the basic necessities we depend on today—I also spent time with very wealthy, lonely people. One shared how miserable she was, as she didn't see a way out of the impossible situation, she'd constructed for herself. She shared her pain and suffering of how she had been wronged by life, despite her large trust fund, and was clearly caught in the pain of her past. She was so attached to her pain, she was so afraid to let go of the huge weight she was carrying around in her mind, which left very little room for anything else. She was stuck waiting for some external sign to guide her.

Listening to her for years, I realized that until she was ready to release this story, all I could do was be patient and listen. It was premature to ask her how long she planned to carry her wounds around, and whether she had any intention of ever releasing them. We can't disregard the past, but when we're ready to face our trauma, we can come to terms and be at peace with some of the wounds and injustices. They brought her to this point, but it wasn't necessary to carry them everywhere she went. But at some point, I withdrew from these conversations, as I could not handle listening to this same story every time we spoke. It was not my work to do, and I needed to protect my own energy. To heal our wounds, we must have the courage to face up to them.

We tend to value what comes from outside ourselves, never recognizing the beauty within us. Own your breakthroughs. Own your mindset. Own your awareness. Own your true beliefs and appreciation for the power you were given to choose a healthy mindset. It's easy to blame someone else for practically everything in our lives, but this does not need to serve us anymore. We give up a bit of our power every time we blame someone or something outside of ourselves for what's happening in our lives. We don't need to compete or keep score, as this takes away our power and hands it to someone else. Each of us is here to have our own experience. There's no reason to compare our life with anyone else's. Claim your power. Keep your heart open to all of the experiences and roads that you choose to embark on.

WHAT ENERGY SOURCE ARE YOU PLUGGING INTO?

Recognize how you spend your time and who you spend it with. If you spend all day on the couch consuming television programs, you will become part of the audience that is receiving and consuming someone else's messages and ways of thinking. If you become a marathon watcher, eventually you will be owning and acting from their belief system. It also gives you very little time to yourself to sit and reflect. It will numb you into a fantasy world, unless you stay mindful as an observer and only take in the information that serves you. Otherwise, you will not develop a healthy understanding of your relationship with knowledge—or reality.

As we will explore in *F*ck the Bucket List for the Health Conscious: Trusting Your Heart*, universal law teaches us that healthy people flow and don't need to control others or the environment. The more you fight the current system, the more you are guaranteed to lose. When you get real with the opportunities in front of you and create, the more you evolve into a healthier existence. What if instead of being the first or the best in a crowded market where everyone craves the spotlight, you dedicated your life to becoming a healthier version of yourself?

Reclaiming your power often brings up your insecurities and vulnerabilities. It can paralyze you and habitually return you to focusing on the old wounds and problems. Sure, we all have challenges that arise, but how you approach them is key. There are many painful and challenging times in every person's life, but how you react is how you wield your power. You can see it as an opportunity to reinvent yourself, or you can run and hide and resort to be a victim. It's impossible to move forward and grow unless you cut the umbilical cord to our suffering. Otherwise, you'll find yourself being fed by the pain of your past, which only creates a very unhealthy state of existence.

Worry, hurt, and fear are emotions we all have, no matter what age we are. No one has a pain-free or worry-free existence. You do have, however, the ability to understand these emotions and the capacity to learn how to use them in a healthier way. Like living in harmony with the elements of nature and the flow of the seasons, you can accept that you have the power to work with them and not be held hostage by suffering. Being at peace and choosing kindness can help determine the quality of your life, especially when you're loving and compassionate with yourself. Just like a wound or scratch, when you leave it alone, it will heal naturally—but if you constantly pick at it, it will take time to heal and no doubt leave a scar.

Poet Kenneth Rexroth reminds us that "maturity is having the ability to escape categorization," and that's the opposite of the conventional wisdom. For many people, the process of growing up and becoming an adult means trying to fit in and be responsible and stable. Rexroth, however, suggests that when we fully ripen into our potentials, we transcend standard definitions. We don't adhere to others' expectations; we're uniquely ourselves, beyond all labels and boxes. "Love slays what we have been, that we may be what we were not." What's your opportunity to practice and cultivate this sacred practice by trekking into the unknown?

EXPEDITION 12

MIRROR, MIRROR, WHAT THE HECK HAPPENED?

From the time we're born, the adults around us do their best to raise us into functioning human beings. More often than not, parents try to avoid the mistakes their parents made with them. They try to prepare us for life, and ask the cliché question that is asked of most children: "What do you want to do when you grow up?"

Grown-ups believe we're doing our best as parents and guardians. We want to make sure our children's dreams are not some kind of fantasy that will be unable to pay their bills and support their adult lives. The adults want to make sure we choose a profession that will ensure financial stability and success. We learn that playing is part of childhood—not the lifelong practice of a responsible adult.

As we grow up, we're constantly bombarded with these expectations. The path we're told to follow is defined by society, handed down from one generation to the next. Too often, as we find ourselves on a track called "growing up," we may feel there is no room for ourselves in the story that has been constructed for us. Even before we're born, preparations are made to shape *who* we will be and *how* we will be. When we arrive, family, friends, and society start to compel us to do certain things in the name of knowing what is best for us.

WHO IS YOUR MIRROR TRULY REFLECTING?

There is a voice of longing inside each of us. We do our best to be good children, good students, good brothers, good sisters, and good friends. We learn to strive for unrealistic levels of success, and that, in order to be the best, we must become the best in the world. But instead, it may leave us overwhelmed, burned out, stuck, and discontent. We may examine our lives and wonder how we got here, and why the stories we were told didn't bring about our ultimate utopia. But we had also learned to quickly silence our questions, as the voices of authority taught us to be quiet and obedient. We were told to be grateful for what we've got and hide our disappointment, even from ourselves.

For many years, I denied my own discontent. I followed the rules and achieved more and more, getting to the so-called top of the game, but felt a vast emptiness from a world that I never really fit into. I tried a lot of different things—from marriages to a successful career—but was underwhelmed when I became conscious of the huge toll they were taking on my soul. Deep inside, I knew that I didn't come here to suffer or chase success and fill my house with more material things. There was something fundamentally distorted with the stories I was told about love and life, but I kept going down the path I was told would bring me fulfillment. And then, one day, my questions became louder and I could no longer suppress them.

I started to realize there were different voices inside of me—some were my own, while others were from my parents, teachers, grandparents, or other figures who brought their own wounds and scars into my life. It took a great deal of work to identify the source of these beliefs, and whether they were actually mine. And then, when I was literally trekking into the unknown, deep in the bushes of the Amazon Rainforest, facing my fears—I saw myself. Not the person I projected to the world, but who I was deeply protecting from within. I saw my fears, my limiting beliefs, and my social conditioning. It was as though a movie played out with each step I took while walking down the undefined paths of the jungle, asking me whether I was living the life I imagined as a child.

It was my own voice—the one I had buried and silenced under a lifetime of cultural conditioning, numbing addictions, and limiting beliefs. This was the voice of the young girl I had been before the world told me who I needed to be. Going to the Amazon Rainforest was never on my bucket list, as I shared in *F*ck the Bucket List for the Soul*, but I did promise myself that if I took this crazy trip, I would do my best to leave my unhealthy fears to compost in the jungle.

I was trekking into unknown territory, where I decided to stop abandoning myself and instead step away from everyone's expectations of how my life should be. Throughout my entire life, I unconsciously rejected the manual of success by firing myself from a successful career and walking away from two marriages, a few partnerships, and my doctorate degree.

I sat for hours staring out at the sprawling trees, plants, insects, and rivers in the jungle and started to hear the whispers of my heart. I decided that I could no longer live in a world that divides me into good and bad or right and wrong based on someone else's beliefs and judgements of how the world should be. I quit being *good* in order to be *healthy*. I was no longer going to please and take care of others at my own expense. It was time to live my life and have the reflection I saw in the river not be about how good or bad I looked physically but be a reflection of my soul. It was definitely not an easy task, because I hated looking at my reflection and regularly avoided mirrors, but it became a daily practice of breathing and smiling more with ease. This was my wake-up call. I was here to live fully and navigate my own internal compass. And I continued on this journey, from expedition to expedition, to discover the brokenness and wholeness within me.

This is a journey for each of us, with different expeditions, that sparks our willingness to bring our full self to face our challenges and opportunities. It's a story of how you can begin to trust yourself enough to know what's healthy and toxic for you, set boundaries, make peace with your body, mind, and soul—as well as your ancestors. On this adventure, you learn to honor your anger, heartbreaks, and disappointments by learning forgiveness for what you didn't have the capacity and ability to know when certain events took place in your life. This is an opportunity of a lifetime to unleash your truest and wildest instincts so that you can be brave and courageous enough to create the healthiest life you can experience. You really deserve nothing less!

FROM THE BEGINNING, LIFE IS DIFFERENT FOR EACH OF US

We come into the world with our own unique gifts that we may not be aware of initially. When we're kids, we're pure and comfortable within ourselves, but as we learn how to crawl, walk, and talk, our outside world starts comparing us to everyone else, attempting to make us "normal" so we can fit in properly as successful humans.

What you find out, at your own pace, is that no one can give you the recipe for how to live your life. You can only conduct your own journey and learn the lessons as they show up. Utopia comes from within. You can find it when you get in touch with yourself, when you're comfortable with yourself, and when you're able to connect to your feelings honestly and without judgment—whether they're happy, sad, loving, or fearful. It's when you have complete acceptance of these states within yourself that you experience profound unity, balance, and harmony by integrating the deep divisions within yourself.

The world can change when you shift your perspective and realize you are on an inner journey and the adventure is personal. It's your biggest opportunity to explore within so you can become whole and learn to fully trust yourself—and only then, connect and trust others. You can also become aware that it's not your fault that you made mistakes or "failed" along the way and forgive yourself. From a young age, most of us have been taught to trust others, especially authority figures and older people, more than our own instincts. When we experienced our parents fighting from an early age, and then that rage turned to us, we learned to comply with how the world in our home played out. And when we are older, we may have had relationships with abusive people until we were able to break the cycle of pain and abuse. How could we have known any other way when we weren't brought up in a musical?

We each have our own path with challenges and opportunities calling our names. How we react to every situation matters, and so does how we pay attention to the lessons that life is here to teach us. Of course, there are days, and sometimes weeks, when reality challenges us to the core, yet it is important to realize it is an opportunity to learn.

Author Paulo Coelho observes that, when we walk in a forest, we'll experience many different trees along the path. No two leaves on hundreds of trees are alike. And no two journeys, along the path, are alike. In his book, *The Alchemist*, he writes, "We are travelers on a cosmic journey, stardust, swirling and dancing in the eddies and whirlpools of infinity. Life is eternal. We have stopped for a moment to encounter each other, to meet, to love, to share. This is a precious moment. It is a little parenthesis in eternity."

Much can shift when you realize that no one has your answers, no matter how hard that person tries to convince you. While we're all connected more than we realize, each of us is here to learn our own lessons and experience our own journey. This can be a time of deep questioning and self-awareness for you, as no one can know what makes you tick better than yourself.

RECEIVING AN EDUCATION FROM LIFE ITSELF

English writer and philosopher, Aldous Huxley, left us a lot to reflect on in his book, *A Brave New World*, regarding his philosophies on our collective responsibility to the planet. Huxley feared a society that would give us so much choice that we would be reduced to passivity and egotism, and that the truth would be drowned in a sea of irrelevance. His body of work is a constant reminder that changing the world is a bit of an arrogant belief to uphold, as our real job may be simpler. He shared, "I wanted to change the world. But I have found that the only thing one can be sure of changing is oneself."

We live in interesting times. We give more value and emphasis on the latest trends and keeping up with technology, frantically purchasing state-of-the-art gadgets and apps that are flooding the markets at ever-increasing speeds. Innovation is all around us, and yet too many dream that their innovative solution will make them rich and successful. And with recent global events, many just want a way to support our lifestyle, not always questioning whether we're aware of what we really need (our *enough*) so we can have whatever lifestyle that supports us instead. One day, we may wake up to the fact that we've been treating what is scarce—like natural resources—with a mindset of abundance, and what is abundant—like opportunities to create and connect—with a mindset of scarcity. No wonder it's challenging to be a young person today. No wonder our world is fragmenting. We have created unspoken assumptions that govern how we live.

If someone told you in 2008 that you could someday get into a stranger's private car, and that stranger would have your credit card information, you probably would not have believed it. And yet, in many major cities around the world, we now trust strangers to transport us from point A to point B, and many parents entrust our children to ridesharing drivers as a safe transportation option.

Businesses like Uber and Lyft sprung up under the brand marketing tool called the Sharing or Collaborative Economy, but we have to look deeper to understand its sustainability and its long-term impact. Look further under the layers, and we find that while these services do provide sharing services—in that local drivers use their cars to drive passengers—not much has really changed when it comes to commoditizing the worker and making the people at the top wealthy.

There is a lot of talk about the wisdom of the crowd, but in this scenario, it does not seem necessarily true because the *sharing* economy has been constructed within the old paradigm in which few know how to truly collaborate and share. While there are advantages, we continue to construct organizations and businesses whose mandate is to compel the public to be consumers of more and more products and services that are deemed innovative. The world is calling the courageous adventurers to step into the new world and truly create and consume the systems that serve all of us by making conscious choices.

The world is changing as fast as these trends, and it is even more necessary to delve into the wisdom of how we address the needs of people in a fair and just manner. Huxley predicted that our societies would become trivial as the pursuit of ego and personal power accelerated. The demise of companies like WeWork and Theranos are sad examples that there are psychopaths and narcissists leading some organizations, and even governments, around the world. Our systems reward those who seek never-ending power with wealth, and, in the systems we created, wealth equals never-ending power. It naturally attracts the sociopaths, the psychopaths, and the narcissists. We allow their power of holding esteemed positions in our society— like leading organizations or celebrating their philanthropy—to manipulate us as they amass more wealth and power.

According to a study dating back to 2010 called, *Corporate Psychopathy: Talking the Walk,* there were at least three times as many psychopaths in executive or CEO roles than in the overall population. But more recent data by forensic psychologist, Nathan Brooks, found it's now a much higher figure: *20 percent.* A 2017 UK study by Kevin Dutton found that companies with leaders who show "psychopathic characteristics" destroy shareholder value, as well as corporate culture. And why do we trust them to have our best interest at heart? Regardless of the state of their mental health, why do we celebrate the billionaires, athletes, actors, philanthropists, and so many others who are deemed successful, at our own expense?

I have worked with incredibly wealthy and celebrated "leaders" during my career, and I always wondered what motivated them to show up every day to work. Some were committed to the purpose of the organization and were there to do their work, while others were there to grab more power, more money, and to feed their egos. It was always at the expense of the people under them, making decisions with limited empathy and concern for the impact on their people.

Their hold on power guaranteed silence. And yet, we are the ones who can decide who we trust, who is healthy and unhealthy for us, and who holds our power. We can step out of the villain and victim stories we've created, simply because we can take the first step.

There is something deeply curious about relying on billionaires—or anyone, for that matter—to save us or the world. As philanthropists continue to wield their increasing power, we can become aware that we're living in their world more than ever, and it's worth asking if that's healthy or toxic. We've constructed a world where, when our governments fail, philanthropists step in to save us from ourselves by offering up sizable donations—at which point, we further celebrate their generosity. Their donations legitimize them as our heroes, which takes the focus away from scrutinizing their practices and whether they're healthy for the world. Why should we believe that a billionaire's "charity" reflects what is needed most by the vast majority of humanity?

Why does poverty, hunger, and access to clean water continue to be a problem? Why doesn't every mother, anywhere in the world, have access to safe birthing facilities and support? Why do we continue to focus only on humanity's biggest problems and not our biggest opportunities? How do we break these cycles? Much can happen when we choose to come together to address our greatest opportunities—and do so in much healthier ways than we could have ever imagined. We have firsthand evidence and experience that this is all possible, should we choose to trek into the unknown and ask the tough questions.

There have been those who walked the Earth before us who called it like it is—such as the philosopher, Krishnamurti, who pointed out, "It is no measure of health to be well-adjusted to a profoundly sick society." When we're "well-adjusted" to societal programming, it's hard to see what's real and what isn't—which is why, at first, we must question everything. Until we do, we continue to play a part in the system, doing what is expected of us, which is deemed honorable. We are expected to accept that there is a certain percentage of psychopaths who run the world. Even worse, we are expected to give them the power to take us in the direction they want to go. But the question we wrestle with regarding our own light and power has been presented to us by many sages, and the answer lies within us.

In the pursuit of profit and being the best, we have lost touch with what is truly valuable in life. The Western philosophy has been overtaken by ambitions of being seen driving the coolest car, owning the latest smartphone, adorning the hippest handbag, hanging out with society's best and brightest, and eating at in-vogue restaurants. Sites like Facebook and Instagram provide a platform for people to share photos and messages. We experience people vacationing in luxury resorts, encouraging others to mediate, and "activists" telling us it's time to lock arms and rage against the system with more outrage. And then there are the reality TV *stars* popping up everywhere, who feed on our attention as they try to increase their ability to cash in on their influence.

In our current reality, battlegrounds are drawn to keep us divided, while for brands, the battle is being fought over our wallets. In many cases, the big companies are swallowing the small in pursuit of economic efficiency. This world we live in was constructed with a great deal of illusion and delusion. There's no doubt about that, as we look around and see the failing systems being challenged and heroes stepping up to save us or make us better. Isn't it time to question where and who we place our faith in so we can trust *ourselves* more fully? The "noise" that someone has your answers is borderline absurd, and the more you understand that, the more you'll be able to move into your own power. It's your choice to decide what you need most and not buy into whatever is being relentlessly sold to you today.

What if what you desire doesn't exist yet and you're being called to create it? This uncharted territory is asking you to step out of your comfort zone. You may be witnessing the deep holes and tears in the safety nets—governments, healthcare, education, financial, and legal systems—you were told would protect you. Maybe being forced to face yourself will release you and no longer hold you back from understanding what's truly healthy for you. Maybe this is an opportunity to take a deep breath and imagine how powerful you truly are?

THERE'S NO ONE COMING TO SAVE US

Human behavior is fascinating, especially our conditioning that the answers to our questions are outside of ourselves. Looking for our answers in some spiritual guru, politician, motivational speaker, philosopher, or celebrity often leads us into massive disappointment. Their words may speak to us, but when their words don't match their actions, all we're left with is the emptiness of a charismatic person who has learned how to draw us into their stories while they grab as much as they can out of us. Whatever it is we may be seeking will rarely be found in a person selling us his or her platform. Spiritual healers or celebrities, focused on their own success, will most likely not have any of our answers, especially when they prey on hopeful people. They may be helpful, to a point, but they're just as much on their own journey as you are. When you become aware of who is healthy and toxic for you, you develop a discernment of who is for you and who isn't and realize that your answers are very personal.

Society, in its current form, is dying from groupthink and consensus, as is our world. Our systems are breaking right in front of us, and instead of stepping out of these systems to invent healthier, more relevant ones, most continue to dispense Band-Aid solutions.

Every living being dies at some point. It is the law of the universe. And the time is now to truly feel who you are and step out as a powerful creator on this planet. Life is not happening *to* you. You are not a character in a television show or a play. It's all real and happening right now, right here, in vivid colors, sounds, and images.

Somehow the personal development of humanity is being left behind in these business models and technologies. More is not always better. The most important innovative designs and leadership needed from people is to remember that you have a voice, and let your own feet do the talking. Instead of automatically following the crowd and buying into what others assume we need, can you see what's truly driving you? Are you courageous enough to navigate towards what is healthiest for you?

Dr. Stephen Covey—American educator, author, businessman, and motivational speaker—reminds us, "Putting first things first means organizing and executing around your most important priorities. It is living and being driven by the principles you value most, not by the agendas and forces surrounding you." When you become self-aware that you are in charge and you are a creator, you can take back your power. What is meaningful to you? What values are important to you? What is it that you want to create, and with whom? You may feel alone, but you are never alone when you have clarity and remember you can turn down the volume on the ever-increasing noise of the world.

UNCERTAINTY IS PART OF LIFE

You can see uncertainty as terrifying or you can see it as an exciting opportunity to explore. Routines give us a delusion of security, comfort, and predictability. While it's good to have a plan, life does not always comply. As legendary English Beatle John Lennon so aptly put it, "Life is what happens when you are busy making other plans." A simple example is: You're running late for an important meeting at the office. You take the same route you take every day, and today of all days, your exit on the highway is blocked. There are police officers signaling that you cannot enter and must follow the road. You've never taken this road before. What are you going to do? The exit is closed and you can't drive through the barrier and your GPS cannot be programmed while you're driving. And the meeting time remains the same.

You can allow yourself to slowly be poisoned by the illusion of the safety of a routine. When you're stuck in a routine, you can never learn anything new or develop skills, which will make it tough to navigate around roadblocks when they cross your path. It's about managing your emotions and acknowledging that getting stressed out by challenging situations is not the answer. When things are out of your control, you can either freak out or you can take a deep breath and imagine other possibilities. You can understand that the person or people you're meeting with have been in similar situations, so what is that you can do? Can you see the opportunities in front of you?

Many of us are terrified of uncertainty because we are being bombarded on a daily basis to create certainty in order to find happiness. Yet, this shuts down creativity, spontaneity, and flow. We can't travel far when we're surrounded by roadblocks or are deafened by someone else's voice.

Life truly is remarkable. When you strive to be at the center of the party or the stage, it's mostly an illusion, as it can only last so long. You'll need to keep grabbing attention to stay at the center. Or, you can learn to be the center of your own story and deal with the punches life will throw your way. The promise of a constant state of happiness is an illusion that does not exist in this reality. And the fear of a constant state of unhappiness, or misery, can be a story you get stuck in. Life gives you lessons, and it is up to you to have a desire to learn without focusing on a destination. Your experience of life will constantly change and evolve, just like nature does.

Inhale deeply and allow all the blessings that surround you to enter your body, mind, and spirit. Let this air fill every cell of your being. Then slowly exhale, projecting calmness, harmony, and peace in your own way—whatever it means to you. Repeat this as many times as you need. Modify it to suit your needs and who you are becoming. To live is to experience all of life, not just sit around contemplating the *meaning* of life. Life is messy, and so are relationships. We can become aware of boundaries—not just our own, but those of others. With experience, we learn to navigate the fragile threads that bind us to each other.

When we're at the beach, there is magic happening right in front of us. When the tide comes in, the sand creates beautiful patterns. This creation takes place as the sand surrenders to the wave and does not concern itself with whether the tide is high or low. It's ready to accept the flow and shift, with grace, to adapt to the next pattern that emerges. There is a beautiful, immersive relationship taking place that is in flow and is whole. Have you ever observed trees during a storm? Like sand, they ebb and flow with each gust of wind that comes their way. They do not fight the wind; they become one energy flow. Some branches may fall off, and some trees will not withstand the storm and come crashing down. There are relationships in nature to learn from that are fluid and show us what alignment is all about.

Learning to disconnect from the external pressures of the world can be a daily practice rather than a programmed detox. Many people get their power from others and the environment, but it's our inner self that gives us the real power we're seeking. Self-awareness helps us disconnect from other people's dramas and shenanigans. It's essential to find that calm place inside ourselves to release our own voice to speak and energize us at our core. We cannot ignore our own darkness, as darkness exists in every human being on the planet. Ignoring it won't make it go away; it will only feed itself on our limiting beliefs of why we can't take action.

For millions of people around the world who suffer from a mental health issue, the manual recommends working with a psychiatrist, taking prescription drugs (and enduring their side effects), and overall ignoring or suppressing the real pain with medication. Something is just not healthy with this story. There has to be another way to treat illness other than by sidelining and bombarding the physical body with chemicals, begging the question: Are we the ones demanding the standard of normalcy be controlled by medication? Have we given up on people because we don't like the way they show up in the world, or because we've lost the patience to tolerate differences? Have we forgotten to look inside ourselves, so that we can look at others with more compassion? If we don't understand ourselves, how can we possibly understand each other?

HAVING BALANCE AND FINDING OUR OWN FLOW

Our hearts and our minds can find a sense of harmony when they have inner dialogues that reach a common ground. We listen to our parents as a child, but as we get older, we can listen more to our own mind and heart. At some point, we can choose to let go of the apron strings and trust our own intuition and not someone else's manual— or, conversely, we can let idle gossip influence us.

Gossip, like news programs, is dangerous and addictive. By its mere definition, it spreads rumors and bad news at the expense of others, and someone is always hurt. It also causes worry and shifts the focus of the mind to what others are doing, when we really should be more concerned with ourselves, not the affairs of others. It's the antithesis of being in touch with our inner self. Many people occupy themselves with worries and concerns about what others think about them. Chasing the latest fashionable trends comes from idolizing those we put on a pedestal, because we give them authority over our society. This means our focus and energy becomes more externalized and distracted, which ultimately empties our inner self.

Gossip is constant chatter stuck in a loop, kept active by exhaustingly talking about someone and their drama. The loop is never-ending and, in fact, snowballs unless we decide to stop and be prepared to reflect. Why are we attracted to this person, or what he or she is saying about our life? And what can we learn about ourselves through this need to participate in drama?

It can be hard to disengage and be quiet. But when we do, we'll discover what we need for ourselves in the moment and examine what this gossip is providing or avoiding. There's so much beauty and joy in self-knowledge; spending time exploring truth is ultimately more meaningful than being engrossed in discussing the affairs of others. It is merely a distraction from attaining a deeper understanding of reality. Just like looking into a book for information—but instead, look into a mirror and see what the reflection is for you.

LEARNING HOW TO NAVIGATE YOUR OWN OPERATING SYSTEM

Healing takes place in the sharing of true knowledge and through revealing hidden secrets buried deep within. Secrets weigh a lot and can be a challenge to keep. There are many different types of secrets: family secrets, clandestine affairs, gambling, addictions, minor and major infractions of the law, dishonesty in the workplace, and the list goes on. They usually are the beginning of lies, fear of repercussions, and embarrassment, or will lead to negative consequences, so they fester and take great effort to keep hidden.

When we're on the path of self-awareness, it's all part of the cleanse to make room for a healthier way of life. The world is mired in a myriad of deception and keeps us separated from the path of creation. We can be bold and imagine and strive to create our ideal world into existence. When energies become stuck, they can hold us back, and we become stagnant. It's up to us to clear out what's no longer working while bringing new life and vigor to any aspect of life that is calling us.

How many times in your life have you had to face challenging times? With 20/20 hindsight, weren't they all valuable lessons that somehow made you stronger and gave you more clarity to navigate where you are going? The more you learn, the more there is to learn. It is a never-ending adventure—the trick is to allow these lessons to be exciting exercises, not something you need to suffer through.

Notice whether you can step out of an unhealthy relationship, for example, and not let the drama possess you. Can you focus on what it came to teach you, so you can learn your lesson? I can sit here and beat myself up for trusting the "wrong" people who did not live up to their word, or I can recognize that they were doing their best but were simply not healthy for me and move on. It's not always easy, because I found myself falling in love with the stories that people have told me when I first met them, only to be heartbroken when I realized they were mostly hot air. These lessons came to teach me about trusting my intuition. I hear my friend, Bill, constantly whispering to me in these situations, "God has 7.7 billion backup plans; it's not all on your shoulders," and it helps me take myself and life less seriously.

The truth of the matter is that we have been deeply programmed. In the societal pursuit of happiness, we have each lost pieces of ourselves. Have you ever noticed how we have been programmed for "success," and yet so much of the focus is on what we're lacking? We have been handed mantras and self-actualization practices to find that elusive happiness within ourselves. While part of humanity continues to be on a path of self-destruction with increased hatred and division, the warring that is taking place is happening within us. When we're joyful, we know it, and don't really have time to stand in front of our mirror and sell ourselves on our positivity.

Our false sense of success conditioned us to want to accomplish everything we can on our bucket list. Otherwise, why are we here if not to achieve? People from around the world travel to the Himalayas every year, dreaming of reaching the Everest summit and checking it off their bucket lists. There are people standing in line and paying more than $50,000 to climb to the top of Mount Everest, one the highest mountains on our planet. And people are literally dying as they pursue this coveted, must-have bucket list item. A feat not just for the best, but for almost anyone with a bucket list. Why doesn't a higher sense of self-awareness ever make it to the top of things you want to achieve in your lifetime, as much as being seen as a winner?

Self-aware people gravitate toward the direction where wisdom comes from. Life is a beautiful opportunity to explore why you are here, and you can change your course when your dream no longer speaks to you. Only you have the ability to evaluate a situation and know what is in your heart. A question to ask yourself is, "Why do I want to do this? Am I doing it because I want to, or because I am expected to?"

BUT WHAT IF THERE IS ANOTHER WAY?

Popular and iconic sci-fi television shows, like *Star Trek*, have tried to show us how we can go beyond this reality. They help us imagine that there is more to the story that we've been born into. At the beginning of each episode, Captain James T. Kirk says, "Space: the final frontier. These are the voyages of the starship Enterprise. Its five-year mission: to explore strange new worlds. To seek out new life and new civilizations. To boldly go where no man has gone before!"

Isn't it interesting that we're off to explore space in our imagination, and yet, there is still so much that is unknown and mysterious on planet Earth? There are millions of people trying daily to convince us that they have our answers and want us to follow their paths and formulas. They want us to consume whatever they are offering. If we close our eyes and imagine a market full of people tempting us with their offerings, we can feel how overwhelming and confusing it is to be here, on this planet, right now.

We've been taught how to distinguish between "right" and "wrong" in order to be successful in our lives. We're taught to respect the past and plan for the future. These are all honorable practices given to us by people with good intentions. The legal system that we're a part of is here to support us, and yet most of our systems have been built around the lowest common denominator—to protect us from bad people with evil intentions, who will most definitely harm us. In the foundation of our human-made systems are fear and the false perception of safety. We may think that the vendors only want attention or money, but in reality, they are after shaping our bodies, minds, and spirits. Some may be good, some may be bad, and the reason we may be so stressed is because we're trying to distinguish between those who may harm us and those who may heal us, and the lines have been blurred.

And yet, we don't have to play the role of a character in the story we were born into. Because, again, our parents and their parents did the best they could with what they knew. For example, the people who came before us were the ones who invented the concept of work, the stock market, the political systems, the education systems, the institution of marriage, and even the concept of having a bucket list.

Let's do an exercise. On a blank piece of paper, create six columns, one each for the following: right, wrong, good, bad, inappropriate, appropriate.

Then write down everything that you can think of that is determined by your society, culture, religion, nationality, and anything else that is external to you, and categorize them in the aforementioned columns. List as many things as come to you.

Now, take a breath and go do something else for a minute. Don't look at what you wrote down yet.

On a fresh page, create the same six columns for the same categories, but this time write down anything that relates to *you* and *your* life.

Then, pull out another fresh page and create two new columns: healthy, toxic. Repeat the task above by writing down external items and, on the back of that page, write down everything that pertains to you personally.

Now, step away and take another deep breath. Take a look at what you wrote for each column and write down your three observations and insights.

We are prone to taking inventory of our past mistakes. We weren't awake or conscious enough to make the best decisions for ourselves, and we subscribed to truths and chose relationships and positions of work that were flat out unhealthy. We can easily use the past as an excuse for our current lack of trust in ourselves.

When our current reality doesn't work anymore, we're experiencing deviance—a simple shift in perspective that is preparing us to create something new. To accomplish this, our path must be allowed to constantly change. When past beliefs are perceived in a healthy light, that doesn't mean they were wrong. We're only seeing evidence of how much we've changed. That, in and of itself, should give us comfort. We're actually continuously expanding as a soul!

So why waste valuable energy judging our past decisions as the basis for not moving forward now? Our newfound intuition is only evidence of the radical movement our soul will continue to experience on this planet. So, who do you trust? Who trusts you? And what is your relationship with trust?

EXPEDITION 13

WHY ARE WE FIGHTING?

We can believe what we want to believe, but at the end of the day, when we understand that there is no destination in life, just life itself, and that no one truly knows us, we become aware that everyone is making up their own stories. From an early age, we are taught to seek the truth in a society where we are often fed lies—even about our history. We no longer understand what's real and what's fake, let alone what's healthy and what's toxic for our bodies, minds, and souls.

We may talk about empathy, but do we truly put ourselves in someone else's shoes and, without bias, understand another's perspective?

Imagine, for a moment, you're seeing the world from the perspective of nature. You're a seed that has been planted firmly in the ground, surrounded by darkness. Above you, you feel a sense of

79

warmth and gratitude when you receive water and sunshine and are connected with other seeds and lifeforms under the ground. There's a vast network of intelligence for you to rely on unconditionally. You have no choice but to grow as more water and warmth reaches you. And this warmth you experience makes you curious about its source and, slowly, you push through the soil. You don't really know where you're headed and have no destination in mind.

Now, you're a human being. You're on a walk one crisp spring morning, experiencing the blossoms of flowers and plants emerging all around you. You're amazed at the beauty that surrounds you and the flowers, fruits, vegetables, and trees that are abundantly emerging after months of winter. As you take this walk, are you aware of the pure magic that you're witnessing? Do you appreciate the natural cycles that provide for us, or are you too busy rushing around being efficient, productive, and ticking off items on your lists?

There is beauty in trusting the currents with a deep understanding that nature teaches us to trek into the unknown at our own pace and have faith in the resources of the sun, the water, and the earth. There is abundant beauty in nature's silence, its intelligence, and its daily miracles. Lynnda Pollio, in her visionary book, *Trusting the Currents*, reminds us that "It's something how our fool mind tries to build the future on worry. Why should something terrible happen? I remembered Jenny saying how thoughts make our lives, and decided to remove that fearful thinking, allowing my heart and its love to saturate the moment instead. I figured if we want the best in life, we shouldn't expect the worst from it."

On this Earth, at this time, we've been separated from each other, ourselves, and nature. Most of us have been taught to win at all costs and fight for our lives. But *what* are we fighting for? And *why* are we fighting? These are questions that many of us have started to examine. Is life really about being better as a winner? And what is the prize when we have to keep winning and stepping on others to get to the "top" of the pile?

Many of us are currently facing a time of extreme discomfort trying to navigate through these uncertain times, and it's an opportunity to become aware of the world we live in and the life we want to create for ourselves and every living being on this planet. It is a time of mass transformation that makes many people uncomfortable, and those who feel called will be stepping up to this deep calling. It means letting go of the conditioning and limiting beliefs influencing how we believe our lives should be lived. And at this time, it's not for everyone. Just like this book is only valuable to those who are ready and will most likely be minimized by anyone who chooses to remain in the current story and paradigm. It's just how we roll right now. The old programming teaches us to resist and fear—and yet, many of us are here to create healthier options that function outside of the ones that no longer serve us.

When we start questioning everything, we're able to get to the root. There's always a purpose to someone presenting a different opinion. What if a different perspective presents itself—not for us to fight, but as a mechanism to help us move forward by understanding ourselves better? The seed that transforms into a plant may experience safety and familiarity in the darkness of the earth, but the light and heat of the sun makes the seed change direction and grow.

Dialogue, instead of arguments, is a valuable opportunity to expand our understanding and interact consciously with people who may have opposing views or beliefs. When we're having disagreements in our lives, they often fuel our anger and judgement. *Why can't Dana see how wrong she is?* This is how conflict begins. The resistance in seeing each other, and picking sides, transforms and gains momentum. As it escalates, there's no common ground and no healthy dialogue exchange. Resistance that's met with more conflict creates more separation, division, inequality, and fear—and we remain warring and fighting as though there's some prize or nirvana at the end of the road.

I am consciously training myself to be in tune with how my body responds to resistance, or when I become aware that someone is trying to attack me (often unconsciously), and why. I often listen to the person's perspective, as it tells me a lot about his or her beliefs and hurts. We're not all the same, and each one of us is here for a reason. It's ours to uncover. When someone wants to continue to argue and needs to be right (and not listen or question), I don't fight, as I have nothing to lose or win. I prefer healthy dialogue over battle lines. We can choose to become warriors, or we can choose to put down our swords and fuel our creative energy in healthier ways that reflect why we're here. When you reflect on your arguments, fights, and the resistance that shows up in your life, consider what they are showing you.

Human beings evolve. We learn, we grow, and we transform. We all experience this transformation, and it's the same with plants and animals. Even though we're connected to family, friends, groups, organizations, and countries, we may have learned to feel discomfort with changes to our everyday life and to fear uncertainty. Change becomes something to fear as the sense of our personal control lessens.

When fear becomes widespread, we sense a loss of personal power that often makes us feel helpless. It's important that we become aware and not let this happen, as this is also an opportunity for growth, renewal, change, and evolution. When do you spend time reflecting? Can you observe the values you live by and check your intentions? How can you shift to a healthy connection to yourself, others, and all who exist on our planet?

THE SOLUTION NEVER EXISTS
INSIDE OF THE PROBLEM

"Problems cannot be solved at the same level of awareness that created them." This observation, made by physicist Albert Einstein, directly addresses the shifts we're being called to make in our lives. Are we trying to solve a situation brought about by decades of decisions made out of panic and bypassing our individual need to truly transform ourselves to a healthy way of living?

Isn't it possible that when we begin to take impeccable care of ourselves, we would be more mindful of the choices we're making—be it how what we consume impacts our environment, society, or other external forces? As children, we were rewarded and recognized for solving problems quickly and according to society's expectations. As we matured and entered the workforce, we learned to be rewarded for our society's pattern of recognizing quick solutions. We learned that when we experienced emotional or physical pain, there was a pill or drug to lessen and often relieve the pain quickly. Short-term solutions were the path we were sold on, when there was another path available to us: getting to the root of *why* our heads hurt or *why* our emotions were getting us down.

The choices we've made about what we purchase—and our lack of awareness of whether something is healthy or toxic—have contributed to the growing toxicity in the natural world. Many of us have simply accepted this as a way of life, thinking that recycling is a way to do good for the environment without examining all of our habits and how they impact the physical world. However, toxicity is not only physical—there are mental and emotional toxicities, as well. It's beneficial to understand this when considering solutions.

When we take actions toward short-term solutions, we don't resolve the bigger foundational issues causing the problems. We merely create situations where these problems appear as different types of toxicity in the world. Quick solutions cause us increasing pain because we mostly ignore the root cause of why we're suffering. When we make decisions or changes out of panic or ungrounded fear, we crave instant solutions. Taking care of ourselves is the greatest action we can take right now to keep our immune systems healthy and vibrant, as well as questioning everything and learning how to trust ourselves in harmony—not fear and panic. "But the problem with rules…was that they implied a right way and a wrong way to do things. When, in fact, most of the time there were simpler ways, none of them quite wrong or quite right, and nothing to tell you for sure which side of the line you stood on," writes Celeste Ng in *Little Fires Everywhere*.

We don't have to drag our baggage with us everywhere we go. When we always reach into our past, our life energy becomes rooted in it. You can choose a path of attracting or facing demons in the shadows and beating yourself up by associating with what stagnates—or you can become aware of the power you have to shift your individual thinking process. What type of world do you want to create and be part of? The universe does not make mistakes.

A MOMENT IN TIME

It has been fascinating to observe the coronavirus outbreak around the world in 2020, and I'll address only one aspect of it here. I chose to live in a remote community. The town I live in has a few thousand residents, while the larger town, twenty-seven kilometers away, has fourteen thousand. I'm mostly connected to that city through local online groups, apart from some of my amazing neighbors. Before the pandemic broke out, I was already fairly isolated, only going into town once a week to get supplies. I rarely ate out and started a vegetable garden. I would have thought it was a sweet, sleepy town had I not seen the hurtful posts and exchanges online. It made me realize that it doesn't matter where we live—the division and separation is alive everywhere.

When I started seeing posts about "the *stupid* people who were littering the grocery store parking lots with their wipes, gloves, and masks," I paid attention to the judgement of smart and noble people who know how to conduct themselves, and those stupid, ignorant people who don't. There was no room for error—you were one or the other. You were the terrible person who would go to the supermarket twice in one day to get groceries and not abide by the limits of certain items, or you were the good citizen who was following and obeying the rules.

No one acknowledged the fact that it was we who started to hoard, ensuring there was more than enough for ourselves, and prompting future restrictions to be made by grocery stores as a result. No one accounted for families of six or eight people who needed more flour, bread, milk, or toilet paper, or people who were shopping not just for ourselves but helping those who were too compromised to be in public. I read the judgement, blaming, and shaming in online posts until someone explained that they were simply trying to feed their large families or help neighbors and friends.

There were also amazing and compassionate activities that were taking place, like the man whose family was unable to come home for his birthday. Strangers left him gifts, cards, and a cake on his porch. While my local bakery was shut down, Nancy, its owner, took orders from locals for supplies and left free packages of yeast and sourdough starters outside her shop.

But there were always people policing and judging others—telling us what they believe the rules should be and how we should act. It's so interesting to get to the root cause of where this conditioning stems from and why anyone feels the need to tell another how to be when you're not putting them or yourself at risk. I experienced this deep-rooted fear when I went to the local farmer's market for the first time and this woman decided it was her job to instruct me on how to be. So, I simply thanked her and then continued on my path. I was not going to change her. She was not going to change me. And I am highly allergic to following anything or anyone blindly. In my early 30s I was offered a job with the condition that I change myself. I was told, "We noticed you wear beautiful pant suits, but we require you to wear dresses and skirts." I have to say that back then I was in a bit of shock and declined the offer. The CEO of the company later called me directly and told me I could wear what I wanted, and would I reconsider. I thanked him and said, "First it's how I dress, then it's how I act. I don't think I will ever fit into your culture, and I appreciate we both know this now." I always dreamed of working for such a firm, but the cost was simply too high.

Some of us came to this planet to bring this compassionate and unified energy, where we no longer need to live in conflict. By becoming aware of the current stories on our planet, you can decide whether you want to continue to participate in them or take another road—one that is less known and less comfortable.

What you learn on this journey is that there's much within you waiting to be unlocked. Your intuition knows which influence outside of you is personally toxic or healthy. Now is the time to learn how to trust yourself first. It's time for our celebrity culture, for example, to come to an end by us no longer giving it our attention. What would happen if you started feeding yourself first, instead of feeding egos that are never satisfied and want more of your attention and resources?

LIVING IN FEAR IS HARMFUL TO OUR LIVES

Fear is an energy that can easily pull us into an unnecessary drama. Any time of change can be painful and cause discomfort. Any evolution of change brings uncertainty and a certain level of darkness into our lives because it's asking us to step into the unknown. But it's also a time of deep reflection and knowing so we can understand our mission and purpose for being born in this time of human evolution. As you'll see in our next expedition in this book, this is a time of purging the darkness within us and making space for the possibilities facing us.

What if you came here, into this very life, to learn about self-responsibility and engage in a deeper surrender into life? Terrible things happen to everyone; no one is spared. But how you react, and how you respond to these events, is personal and up to you. Each of us faces our own diverse and unique set of challenges and problems. But what if each challenge provides you with an opportunity to face yourself and others in a healthier way?

Each of us will experience some level of betrayal, suffering, and loss at some point in our lives. And regardless of how "good," empathetic, and compassionate we are, every one of us has hurt someone, at some level. We've each played the role of victim and villain at some moment in our lives. In her book, *The Faraway Nearby*, author, historian, and activist, Rebecca Solnit, writes, "Some people love their story that much even if it's of their own misery, even if it ties them to unhappiness, or they don't know how to stop telling it. Maybe it's about loving coherence more than comfort, but it might also be about fear—you have to die a little to be reborn, and death comes first, the death of a story, a familiar version of yourself."

Once you can step out of unhealthy stories—which is the test—you can meet each challenge by seeing and experiencing who you truly are. The trap is staying within these roles and living them over and over. The opportunity is to see and experience who you are, and who you choose to be, so you can create healthy stories. You have an incredible ability and capacity, when you tune fully into yourself, to recognize the wide range of choices in how you respond to every situation and your freedom to choose. Isn't this why so many of us have spent our lives yearning for freedom from societal prisons of the mind?

Your freedom lies not in controlling what happens to you, but in taking control of how you respond. A celebrity would not be celebrated if we chose not to feed him or her with our attention and our resources. A philanthropist would not be a philanthropist if we didn't provide him or her with a tax receipt for giving our money to "charitable" causes, throw a gala dinner to celebrate the generosity, or applaud when his or her name was posted on a street sign or a plaque on a building. We create all of this, and we decide whether we continue to buy into it.

How we choose to respond matters, as that's what's within our control. Fear and stress bring disease and illness to our physical and mental body. It causes us to divide in a world of right and wrong, where we police each other with judgement, shame, and guilt. It's how we've been hardwired to live, but we have more available to us than we ever imagined when we choose to respond with compassion, humility, and integrity. Regardless of the situations we're facing, and despite our external conditions, we have access to how we respond. Listen to the story of a survivor of sexual abuse, human trafficking, a war, or a concentration camp. Despite being a victim of circumstance, some have been able to create a healthy way of life once their ordeals passed, while others remain victims of their circumstances because their pasts continued to haunt them, which is understandable.

Research from the past few decades has consistently shown that there are many people who would love to quit their jobs because they just can't take it anymore. I fired myself from a very successful career after failing to convince my boss to fire me, despite numerous attempts. But I learned that it's not healthy to make decisions in fear and find yourself scrambling into the unknown. Not everyone has the resources or ability to quit out of fear. We may end up in a similar job or relationship simply because we didn't invest in what we wanted to fill our life within terms of our work. The key is to create a bridge to keep ourselves sane. I spent a great deal of energy volunteering with organizations and joining boards that inspired me while developing new skills that brought forth new opportunities. What's in our control is being able to be curious about our gifts, our talents, and opportunities, and to experiment with where we can put these things into action. When we have a healthy mindset and are open to life, we make decisions aligned with our inner guidance, and not in fear.

We've been taught that we're here to participate in a world where events happen to us. We've also been given tools, frameworks, and practices to navigate this world with indicators that tell us when we're succeeding and when we're failing. But what if we're not just here to navigate our life and the world, but to come into harmony with nature to be powerful creators? What is it that you want to live by, who do you want to create with, and what is it that you want to experience?

WHAT IS YOUR TRUE WORTH?

Many people crave daily routine and the structures we're used to—like going to work, meeting friends for dinner, or going to the movies twice a month. What we often don't realize is that we were born into structures that taught us what to value, such as learning that if we just work hard enough and apply ourselves in school, sports, and life, we can achieve anything and have *the good life*. Were you ever told, "The harder you work, the happier you will be. The harder you work, the more people will value you. The harder you work, the more you will achieve in your life and the more successful you will be"? How close is this to the script that was handed down to you?

It does take hard work to transform an idea or an intention into reality. We don't become a mechanic or a nurse overnight. Books don't write themselves. But does hard work always lead to more achievement? Don't store clerks, cleaners, artists, teachers, and factory workers work hard? Are they acknowledged and respected for their hard work by society? Do they participate in the financial success from the value their hard work brings their employers? And what about people with extreme wealth? There's a belief that when one is wealthy, we have everything, and this why so many aspire to be wealthy as well. Interestingly, a 2017 survey by Illinois-based financial research firm Spectrem Group found 20 percent of investors worth between five million and twenty-five million are concerned about having enough cash to last their retirement. Their work or inheritance led to their wealth, and yet they still fear its value. Does upholding the values of doing *hard* work make sense to you?

Some of the hardest work I have ever done was not for a paycheck— and I have worked in some capacity since I was fourteen years old. But I, like many of us, grew up believing that a job and work will lead to achievements and happiness. The metric taught by society, schooling, parents, and grandparents was to measure ourselves by the yardstick of work. This limiting belief ends up working against us. The number of hours we work, or how busy we are, doesn't truly determine our value.

When you're a worker who is contributing to your own wellbeing, that's simply enough. But when you have to fear how others evaluate you, it may be time to step away from this story. When we feel afraid and disconnected from our inner source, we tend to act out in selfish ways that do not contribute to the health of the whole. In a sense, we separate ourselves, and look for ways to validate our self-worth.

The way we value ourselves is changing. It no longer needs to be a fear of not living up to how hard we work, or any external yardstick. Does it truly matter if people think you're accomplishing less? Busyness is a modern-day affliction, and it all depends on what you value. But many of us no longer want to be robots or slaves to a system that doesn't value us. Productivity and efficiency are not the hallmarks of a soul.

WHAT ARE WE FIGHTING FOR?

The healthier question is, why are we fighting at all? We've been conditioned to fight for our lives. Do you fight for your life? Do you know how to fight? Do you have the skills to fight? Are you winning or losing on your battlegrounds? We are told to *keep fighting*. But *why* are we fighting? What are you fighting for? Does our world really need us to be *warriors*?

Imagine for a moment that you were told to play for your life. What does playing look like? Who would you play with? Do you have the skills to play? When you had a choice, would you keep playing or would you need to keep fighting for your life? What choices are you making to live a healthy life? Can you even remember *how* to play?

When I worked in corporate America, I was part of a very big machine—a large company in Silicon Valley that was winning against our competitors and wanted to continue to win by being number one and crushing the competition. It was a daily race to success with hours of filling out endless templates and making slides. And we did win. As the chief strategy and innovation officer, our team brought Canada to the number one global position, and we won against the other big countries like the UK, Japan, China, and Germany. But what did we *actually* win? Why were we competing internally, as well as in the marketplace? As I went on medical leave after a plane crash, which is a story I will keep for another time, these were questions I started to ask.

The first memory of my life is one of war. I experienced people coming together around shared purpose in the most caring and loving ways, despite the deep threat and uncertainty that we faced. My short life could have come to a complete stop had my side lost the war. What I witnessed, at that time, was a profound connection between people when their survival was at risk and they had a common reason to work together. But I also experienced firsthand that people usually die in a battle zone—on both sides. There is always a cost to winning. For someone to win, someone must lose.

My dream for the world is that we wake up to this reality. I now shy away from people whose goal is to be number one. What useful purpose is it to let people know that you have done something that no one else has done? How does that help anyone? And yet, go to your social media feeds and become aware of the posts you "like" or "heart." Who do you believe is *truly* amazing? What beliefs or people do you give your power away to by supporting their need to win?

I am choosing my words more carefully. For example, it is a daily practice to become aware of when I use the word "better." I want to witness more of us creating *healthier* systems that lift each other up, instead of *better* systems. I look at a person and ask myself, "Is this person healthy or toxic for me?" and I spend time understanding why and what this says about me. It is a journey of awareness—not judgement or blame. I can more easily walk away than stay caught up in someone else's drama.

At the end of the day, life is all about stories. Stories you tell yourself, and stories that you tell other people. Imagine what could happen if we stopped warring and fighting within ourselves, trying to feed the emptiness of being the best and winning at all costs to attain the myth of success. Can you catch yourself when you use divisive words like, "them or us" or "those people," or when you believe one toxic system or person can replace another? Isn't it time to put down the sword and stop fighting? What are you fighting for? More importantly, is it the way you want to spend your beautiful time on Earth?

At the age of three, my sister (who was seven at the time) and I helped our mom cover all the windows of our apartment with black sheets. We were on constant alert to be ready to go to the bomb shelter where we were supposed to be safe. Sirens and radio reports from the outside world governed our lives. I remember one of our neighbors being told that her son had been killed. I can still recall the pain and the deep loss that day. That suffering and loss stuck with me—it made me who I am. It showed me how people come together during times of crisis with clear purpose and intent. I had experienced a sense of community, long before the Internet or social media.

I always wondered why it took an act of violence to bring people together in this way. If you've ever experienced it, you will know that feeling of community, compassion, and caring that prevails in the aftermath of such events. At that moment, there is a deep feeling of togetherness. There is clarity of purpose. The potent emotion that you feel when you experience terror and trauma galvanizes people. It helps us understand how emotion and heartfelt connection to an opportunity inspires action.

What I learned from my childhood is that when people face overwhelming odds, they can come together around a shared purpose with trust and conviction. At the age of fifteen, I found myself being the youngest member of a delegation to Austria, Germany, and Switzerland. I was shocked I was selected, as I was outspoken about the need for peace in the world and the region. I was also part of a local community theatre group that produced a play written by a friend of mine called, *Dolls,* about the Majdanek concentration camp war trials, which was later televised for German and Israeli audiences. I'll never forget bringing local youth together for a memorial I organized at the Dachau concentration camp in Munich that led to hours of deep dialogue and connection. Watching one of our chaperones, a Holocaust survivor, wipe tears off his face as he was haunted by the past while witnessing the present bridges being built to heal us all, helped me understand from a young age that I was here to bring some sense of unity to our world. As I read the poem that I had searched for hours to find for this memorial of all who lost their lives in this genocide, I felt the healing power of words and actions take us into the unknown.

What I learned as I grew older is that history repeats itself in the name of ideology, with every side fighting for its own cause and survival. Had the other side won the war when I was three years old, I would not be here on this path with you—it would have achieved its goal of avenging its martyred brethren. Too often, our enemies have a shared purpose that can ignite our own. This is insanity on a whole different level, based on deep-rooted mutual hatred and fundamentalist dogma.

You can compare your immune system to a Department of Defense. When waging a war, the Defense Department relies on its Air Force, Navy, Army, and specialized intelligence units, antiterrorist teams, and other forces to work together in a coordinated fashion to defeat the enemy. The human immune system operates like a highly efficient killing machine to fend off germs. It employs a variety of strategies and weapons based on the specific threat it faces and uses a complex defensive process to protect us. Your body works hard to repel invading viruses and illnesses, and there is a legitimate need for healthy living and taking care of our immunity.

No one can question how ingrained war is in our world and history. When we choose to turn on the news, images flood into our field of vision of a battle somewhere on the globe. We may feel outrage as we witness these insane reports of the loss of life somewhere close or far, but the cycle continues. We may say "never again," and yet the news keeps bringing us reports of wars from all edges of the world. And with the Internet, these stories are flooding in faster and faster every day.

For some reason, we have brought the war analogy not just into families and relationships, but also into the fabric of business. The competition is seen as the enemy, and the purpose is to win the highest market share or top spot. It is easy to get people to rally the troops and aspire to get the number one market share spot. The deeper question is: Is it necessary to have a shared purpose of bringing down the competition, when today the opportunity is to get people to focus on a shared higher purpose and find ways to collaborate and co-create with sometimes unlikely partners? It is an opportunity to rally people around what your business is doing in the world and why it makes our planet better through our work.

In too many organizations, there is increasing competition *inside* of the organization, where people and departments are battling each other for resources and ownership. So much energy is spent on internal competition, when we can find ways to come together around a shared purpose of creating an incredible offering in the marketplace. There is no reason to crush anyone when we remember *why* we are in business. Imagine what could happen if we brought the art of co-creation and cooperation into the fabric of how business operates. What if, instead of having "war rooms" in organizations, we had co-creation spaces where we brought our internal departments together for a higher purpose that helped our organizations thrive? What if we're here to thrive in our higher purpose instead of winning a game that destroys our own and the planet's wellbeing?

Isn't it time for us to recognize the power business has to shift humanity in a new direction for future generations, to create a healthy path forward with shared purpose? We would no longer need to crush the competition at all costs. We can choose to have more faith in our ability to build and co-create, as we have witnessed what happens when the drive for survival transforms into blind destruction and hatred. There is another way for us to change the mindset of leadership, to co-create a new path to bring back the simplicity and beauty of business. Business can be a force powered by the mission of providing exchanges between people, and working to support each other, our communities, and the planet.

The truth of the matter is that there are two sides to every coin. When we can each understand that it is possible to engage with healthy competition, as much as the unhealthy, we can become conscious of the choices we make. The "unhealthy" separates us and encourages us to win at all costs, while the "healthy" encourages us to compete only with ourselves, so we can grow and flourish. Can you find the harmony within yourself, and let any necessary changes happen in the least harmful way with the most compassion?

Become aware of your need to compete and compare yourself to others. There's always resistance that pushes us forward, as it helps us reevaluate our true purpose. It's an opportunity to understand your level of negative self-talk and where these beliefs of being better than anyone else stems from. The old paradigm programmed us to judge ourselves based on how we compare, based on criteria of perfection and societal conditioning. Imagine if there's no one else to take down or compare ourselves to—how would your life be different? What if the decaying paradigm is set up, by design, to make us feel like a failure? What if you can shift your beliefs about the need to win and let go of any negative self-talk you're having about not being the best? When we trek into the unknown, we not only take risks, we reap the benefits of getting closer to our mission, which can be as simple as living a healthy life.

THERE IS ANOTHER WAY

Here are some suggested questions to sit with—please add your own and make it personal and relevant to you.

- What's your relationship with fear, safety, conflict, and change?
- Is there a war within your body, mind, or soul?
- Is there a war within your physical experience?
- Is there a war within your family?
- Is there conflict in your own relationships?
- Is there division within your systems, institutions, and organizations?
- How do you respond to resistance?

It may seem small or insignificant to be in a disagreement with a friend or neighbor but imagine the ripples from the conflicts that all of us have within ourselves and each other. When we're tied to this negative, divisive energy, we are held within this darkness. When we're giving energy to these divisions and conflicts, what are we creating in our own world and the world outside ourselves? Are you aware of what you're creating?

It's healthy to take a pause. Otherwise, you may be caught in fighting harder and harder, spending your energy on what doesn't work until you ultimately burn out. In times of transformation, and even crisis, you face an opportunity to reframe your situation instead of fighting it. You no longer need to be trapped in the ways you used to react and can shed unhealthy fear, so you can tap into your expansive courage to live a healthy life. When you adopt the mindset of an opportunity creator, you can take the healthy aspects and transform them. As you step into the unknown, are you starting to unravel your own mystery and connect with all of life that surrounds you?

EXPEDITION 14

DECLUTTERING, PURIFYING, AND CLEANSING

Many of us are experiencing instability within the structures that we trusted throughout our lives, but that doesn't mean that we need to revolt or tear down the dying structures in the same way our ancestors did. Our human history, as recorded in our history books, calls for the death of one leader, one regime, one paradigm to usher in a better one. The hunters ultimately become the hunted, and the oppressed become the oppressors. Much energy goes into discrediting the evils of one simply by replacing it with another. And yet, despite all the revolutions, uprisings, genocides, and efforts to save the world, our history simply repeats itself over and over.

This is why the curious adventurers and courageous bridge

builders are being called right now to shift from this designed division to an awareness that there are other paths to carve out. Otherwise, all we continue to do is add fuel to a fire that has been raging for centuries or invest our energy in putting it out temporarily. Now imagine for a moment that you would apply these same acts of violence, blame, and outrage against yourself. Imagine revolting and wanting to tear yourself down. Do you know where this deep sense of destruction and need to fight originates?

Our current reality is filled with contradictions and can be confusing to navigate. It's up to each of us, at our own speed, to become aware of what's in and out of our control and acknowledge that there's a spectrum of opportunity and options that we can choose. The path of freeing ourselves is one we actually get to uncover. Do you want to invite the path of more resistance into your life, or the path of least resistance? They are both challenging paths, and yet we have a choice when we start doing our own inner work through self-exploration, self-understanding, self-compassion, forgiveness, and holistic healing.

As adventurers, humans have explored the moon, distant galaxies, faraway lands, and the depths of the oceans. We are curious about how things work and celebrate our technological innovations and scientific breakthroughs. But how curious are we about exploring ourselves? It is much more acceptable to go to war and annihilate other people in distant lands than it is to understand the source of our own suffering and destruction. We've been conditioned to look in the mirror and only observe our physical image reflecting back at us, wondering if we look presentable enough to the outside world. Psychologist Carl Jung observed that, "People will do anything, no matter how absurd, to avoid facing their own souls." And, indeed, we are experts at strategizing against the enemies *outside* of us and mostly avoid facing the enemies looming *within* us. Our history shows us that it is much easier to blame and be victimized than honestly look within ourselves.

Doing our work requires us to pause, be still, question, and listen before responding and reacting. Becoming conscious—living in awareness—is key to healing our wounds. There's always a feeling deep within us that's calling us, but the question is whether we trust it or suppress it. When a dam bursts, there's a sudden and rapid release of captive water. The same thing can happen to us. When something blocking our energy, removing it can free us from its hold. We have the power to break through—in fact, we are the only ones who can.

We're each currently at our own crossroads; determining whether to take the known or the unknown path. Our mindset charts a large part of our path. Do we perceive a world of struggle or possibility, scarcity or abundance, fear or love, division or unity? Our curiosity influences our willingness to cleanse, purify, and declutter our lives of what no longer serves us—beyond the material stuff, and rather go inside ourselves to get in touch with our whole self. True change begins when we're able to envision something in a healthy light. It comes first from within us and the choices we make, which are only then reflected in our own outer world.

But it's rarely easy to choose a path of transformation. When we declutter our homes of material stuff, we get a sense of how much we've accumulated. And then, we decide which items are still functional and valuable in our life, and which we no longer need. But when we become aware of what products, beliefs, and people we've stuffed our bodies, minds, and souls with, the game changes entirely. The woman who made decluttering trendy, Marie Kondo, goes deeper by advising us to, "Keep only those things that speak to your heart. Then take the plunge and discard all the rest. By doing this, you can reset your life and embark on a new lifestyle."

Trekking into the unknown is about the soul journey and our

ability to imagine and dream. It is so essential that we dream. When we give up dreaming, we give up on our life. Imagining and living go hand-in-hand, because that is where we tap into our purpose, open ourselves up to the mystery of life, and accept who we are and why we're here.

You can only receive the amount of energy or light that you can absorb. You have your own hands on your own dimmer switch, which you can turn up or down. You are in charge of your own switch. When it seems to get too dark, you have the ability to let more light in to shine on you. While the sun shines during the day, it disappears at night. Likewise, there are patterns and cycles in life where we all experience dark moments. Can you become aware of the patterns in order to begin to move through them and out the other side? Remember, it is always darkest just before dawn.

WHAT ARE WE SEARCHING FOR, AND WHY ARE WE SEARCHING?

There are people who are constantly searching for something—whether it is a relationship, a better job, more knowledge, more meaning, more belonging, or more adventure. Sometimes, we can get so busy searching that we forget what we're looking for. The search itself then becomes the focus or goal. It's like the story of the guy who searched the whole world for love, and the person he fell in love with, years later, lived across the road. They only found each other when he stopped searching and started being present in his life. How often do you search for someone or something that is right there in front of you? For some reason, you can't see it, or you are trapped into believing that what you are looking for is lost or challenging to find. Too often, the search and the seeking become everything.

Our mission and purpose transforms into a never-ending desire to uncover more and more knowledge, with no satisfaction in sight. Eventually, we lose ourselves because we become irrelevant in the equation as our focus turns into an obsession of achieving success.

Some days we may find ourselves looking frantically for something that has been right in front of us the whole time. It is in a place that has always been there, waiting for us to see it. In the never-ending pursuit of more, better, or perfect, we too often forget to stop and look around and acknowledge our surroundings right here and now. We can get too caught up in what we may be lacking—compelled by the fear of lack that has been programmed into much of humanity. In fact, the essence of life is simple. It is here to be experienced and enjoyed, not to constantly walk around in circles searching for what we feel is missing. The only moment we have is *now*, to be fully present, and to see and experience the beauty and opportunities around us.

Thankfully, sometimes we let our guard down, collapse from sheer exhaustion, and actually let ourselves rest from all the striving and searching. This is when we let our compassion shine through, as we surrender our persona and crack open enough of our true self to bring forth the parts of ourselves hiding in the darkness. Unless we're willing to acknowledge the dark parts that we may perceive as weakness and keep them buried, we will forever be chasing "the train leaving the station," or stuck on our "hamster wheel." We will never experience the feeling of wholeness unless we include all the parts of ourselves. It is in the experiencing of life, not in the seeking, that our window to the world opens up and expands.

Many of us were born into a world of suffering, which has been ingrained in us since birth. We are expected to uphold responsibilities that are often to the detriment of our well-being. We may be on a path that is completely opposite to what our heart desires. Do you know where you may be restricted the most? Where do the people in your life expect you to uphold responsibilities that they depend on? What role does suffering play in your life? What's your relationship with suffering? How does it show up in your day-to-day experiences? Where do you feel the most resistance, and do you know where it stems from?

Take time to reflect on these questions, and please add your own, until you can get to the root and the source. It may take an investment of time and energy to become aware of what you're carrying within you and why. It may require you to observe some of your most difficult relationships and understand where you feel suppressed or stuck. The key is to uncover and get in touch with your self-compassion and self-love.

When I chose to purge and cleanse deep conditioning and wounds, I often found it challenging to integrate back into the world where things had not changed at the same pace. It was really hard to be around friends and family who expected me to hold the same belief systems and not change. But what I learned is that when you connect with your true essence, you keep expanding and growing, which can become uncomfortable when the people around you stay the course. The main change we experience when we take steps to trek into the unknown is the realization that it may be time to let go. The big discrepancy that took place when I began this journey was that the people around me were living the same life, but I wasn't.

As we clear ourselves of the old programming, we allow space to ask questions and hear our own voices emerge. When we choose this path, it's not easy, as there are abundant paths in front of us. But one of the choices that helps us heal is deciding what we want to bring along on our journey. How heavy is it to carry your fear and anger everywhere you go, and can you lighten your load?

WHAT HAPPENS WHEN WE UNLEARN?

We have been trained to focus on our external world as an indicator of our wellbeing. When we look at our current education system, for example, many of us are starting to see that it's becoming increasingly irrelevant. Young children in nursery and preschool are encouraged to tap into their imagination, which is then largely suppressed and criticized in elementary and high school. Our education systems are failing because they are sending all children in the same direction, with the same constructs and vision. Many children are discouraged from having self-expression as a one-size-fits-all curriculum. History, for example, is being taught as the basis for understanding what's happening on our planet. It keeps us anchored in the past (the known) as the way to predict the future (the unknown), which often further stifles the imagination and curiosity of our children. When we prepare them for jobs (known) by asking them what they want to do when they grow up, we shut off their ability to imagine the future (unknown).

Our education system has played a significant role in creating experts who are validated by the quality of education and specialization received—and yet, anyone who doesn't go through the education system is labeled uneducated and unqualified due to not having the proper "paperwork" endorsing knowledge and experience. Unless we enroll in the *right* schools, we do not have the same opportunities as those certified and educated. Have you ever wondered who designed the military system, the political system, the business system, and whether they are also the brain children behind the prison and the factory systems? It all began somewhere in the bigger system, which then spilled over into the same design and infrastructure for the education system. Someone imagined and created all of this and taught us to accept it as reality.

But what happens when we choose to free ourselves from believing that this current infrastructure is simply the way the world works? What happens when we wake up to this voice inside of us that is questioning everything? How does it feel to become aware that it is us humans who constructed the beliefs, the systems, and the boxes we call reality? It's okay to say, "This is how the world works right now," after observing everything from how war, love, marriage, divorce, employment, taxation, and lawfulness show up on the planet—but it doesn't mean that it has to stay the same. Now, what happens when you observe the constructs and monuments you worship in your own life in the same way as you observe the world? What do you see?

We're each being asked to seriously question what we're personally willing to tolerate and to face our fears and take action to create a healthy foundation for our own lives. Our systems teach us to learn, and we have the opportunity to unlearn and shift. We have so much more than we can even imagine. Imagination is connected to a sense of possibility, shifting away from a mindset of problems and scarcity to a mindset of opportunities and abundance. The current system can be a huge culprit in limiting our creativity and spreading fear that we're feeding on to fill us up. We have an opportunity to unlearn and decommission what we've been fed and taught that no longer resonates with us.

But there are no quick fixes. There is no magic pill or silver bullet. It's about becoming aware of how to trust yourself by unlearning limiting beliefs and habits, to be brave enough to ask deeper-probing questions and not accept the status quo. It's about unearthing an understanding of how you got to where you are—and your own personal perception of who you are—right now in the world. Is this serving you for your highest good? Does this make you feel happy and content? If yes, that's fantastic. And if not, what areas are no longer serving you? Is it the people around you, the beliefs imposed on you?

Or is it the system failing you and breaking down? Only you can see the invisible lines that constrain you and hold you hostage.

So many of the beliefs and assumptions around happiness, success, safety, love, and death are inherited. Our conditioning creates fears around how we succeed or fall short in the eyes of the world to keep up with the current systems. These are the beliefs that need to be examined. I will be the first to admit that this is not an easy task to unlearn or deconstruct. Think about it—it has taken ten, twenty, thirty, forty, or even ninety years to build who we are, and change, change will not happen overnight. However, to start, we must first identify our own invisible prisons, the ones that keep us trapped in systems that no longer serve us.

Where do you begin in reexamining these fundamental assumptions? Can you identify what you were taught to believe throughout your schooling from your caregivers, teachers, parents, and from your culture? For example, the feeling of being compared to others and competing with them for the best grades, friends, and status was a concept impressed upon many of us from the day we were born. The push to get from here to there to feel liked, and be recognized as, a winner and not a loser. The need to always prove that you are good enough or that you are worthy. This is when the accolades and the power of prizes and awards emerge. This is where you can get caught in the trap that you are not good enough. Today, technology has upgraded these conditionings with sophisticated approaches using entertaining apps and software to magnify our shortcomings. The downside of social media is that it creates platforms that celebrate the act of public bragging and unwittingly widen the gap of separation and artificial scarcity.

You can choose to stay in your box, carry around someone else's lunchbox handed down to you, or be creative and reimagine a healthy meal in a brand new one. Life is unique and exceptional to each of us, and it is up to us to make it special for ourselves. Life really is for the living, and it is up to us to nurture our relationship with life. The big question to consider is how *you're* treating life, as opposed to how *life* is treating you.

The idea of unlearning is not new. It is at least four thousand years old and is rooted in sacred texts. There are many amazing stories in our collective history about inspirational people who were self-taught and became pioneers, changing the course for humanity. It is encouraging to know more people today are looking to step out of the rat race. More and more are questioning the fast-food culture we've created, wanting to support different lifestyles that align with abundance and nutrition that is created from the heart—not from great profit margins.

Everything in our home, for example, that has not been genetically modified, comes from nature and someone's imagination. We simply forgot to recognize the source of our materialistic items and to give nature the credit for the abundance it offers us. The national treasures of Shillong, Meghalaya, in northeast India, have amazing living root bridges constructed from the actual living root system from the rubber fig trees. These are spectacular architectural designs that can only be co-created in harmony with nature, taking between fifteen to twenty years to create, and lasting up to five hundred years. They are a constant reminder of the importance of partnering with mother nature to honor her existence. The more connected we allow ourselves to be with the living systems that sustain us, the more we can flow freely and naturally.

In the distorted viewpoint, we believe that to be innovative we must conquer nature and manipulate it for our needs. When we can stop and recognize the insanity of this type of thinking and reconsider that there are possibly natural systems that are trying to show us the way, a lot can happen in this shift of perspective. All this beauty and simplicity is right in front of us every day. When the Khasi and Jainitia indigenous people thought of how they would cross the forest, they looked all around at the natural resources to construct a living bridge that would serve all.

Your body is made up of many integrated working systems and parts. For example, your stomach is part of your digestive system and your liver plays an important role for your immune system. All these different groups serve a higher purpose for the human body to operate at maximum capacity. There is no part of the human body that works alone in isolation; each system has a specific job, with the support of all the organs. In a similar way, it's time for us to collaborate with respect and in harmony to create more innovative systems that honor and follow the cycle of nature. By learning how to become truly healthy, you can explore your own individual roles, which can range from living a healthy life to supporting the whole.

WHEN WE LOOK INSIDE OURSELVES

As you move through these challenging and changing times, be gentle with yourself and others. Unlearning requires us to examine our box and learn a new, healthy way of being. We may decide to stop working so hard and not focus so much on needing to get from point A to point B, the way we were taught. We may choose, instead, to spend more time experiencing our life and our place in the world. This allows us to go deeper inside ourselves and tap into our inner wisdom.

There are so many brilliant people on this planet, and yet we don't know how to play together to make the changes that are so needed without being competitive. One of the reasons is that we have forgotten how to do our own work first. Instead of traveling to a goal or destination, how about taking a journey deep within yourself?

Have a conversation with your intuition about what you know to be true. As the habits and decaying systems on the planet crumble, an opportunity arises for you to put down the manual. Take a chance and step out of your invisible prison to experience the feeling of freedom. Step into nature to reconnect and feel the breeze on your cheeks, the rain on your body, and the sun on your face, and let it guide you to your natural state of creation.

When you truly look at a person, beyond the titles and credentials, you will be able to start shifting into a new world of possibilities to explore. Most of us have more than we can imagine inside of us that we are suppressing. Yet uniformity and conformity have a strong hold, as we have been raised with a unique identity and a craving to belong. We have been taught that we need our country, our city, our sports team, our job, our marriage or relationship status, our property, and our family to define us. Otherwise, who are we? Paradoxically, we often protect and hide our individuality while, at the same time, we yearn to belong to a "tribe" and part of something bigger than ourselves. Whether it is living in subdivisions or our constant pursuit of success, we may have forgotten how to build thriving communities, which share a strong purpose and support the whole.

When relocating to another city, or even immigrating to another country, people look for and seek out others they can relate with. Finding individuals who come from the same culture and communities brings us comfort and connection. For example, remembering a shared neighborhood or discussing local restaurants offers a sense of congeniality that facilitates conversation and connection. However, finding people unlike us opens us up more to life. It may be more difficult to converse, but these unlikely connections can often translate into meaningful ones because they take us out of our comfort zone. We get to experience scenarios and areas where we're confident and where we also lack confidence.

Sometimes it is important to recognize the strengths in others in order to adopt them for ourselves. It allows us to truly connect and create something more powerful.

Children need time and space to grow. This is also true for adults, and even more so for adolescents. We also need real time and space to be free to experiment and explore. Imagine having a few hours each day to freely explore, engage, connect with yourself, and be with others just to be and enjoy. Can you let go of limiting beliefs such as, if you are doing nothing, you are lazy? Why do you have to be in constant motion? Who does it serve? Is our society creating zombies who are sleepwalking through life, in the pursuit of being busy and successful? Why not just lift and shift your mindset to see opportunities and lighten your load? Of course, you may fall down or trip up, but it takes practice and determination to figure out how to free yourself. The key is to see what works for you, and simply start. Listen to yourself and begin.

WHY ARE WE HERE?

We each came to this planet to do something during our lifetime as individuals and as part of a community. First, do you believe you play a role in the collective? Everyone has a purpose and a role to play. The ant and bee colonies are great infrastructures to observe; they are so organized that they can move mountains and destroy forests, all due to working together in harmony and remaining united in their goal.

Ants have incredible defense mechanisms to ensure the safety of all the members of their colony. They also have a way to supervise and house thousands of ants in perfect harmony. A single acre of the Amazon rainforest is home to 3.5 million ants. There is no central power structure featured in the management of any ant colony, but at the heart is the Queen, who does not oversee any of the ants. Every ant has its role and is self-responsible and accountable for its own job. Self-organizing mechanisms are present everywhere in nature. We all have a purpose, but it's our job to realize what it is. No one serves it to us on a platter. When we're not connected to it, we fall off track and, consequently, we start to create our own mess.

When you become clear about your purpose, you find a certain level of inner peace emerge. You will be more grounded, and when you feel grounded, you can begin to help others. Notice how grounded people act and the positive energy they project. When you are not grounded, you are not connected to the earth and therefore feel lost. This creates negative energy and, before you know it, you are swirling in a mess, creating problems and stuck in suffering.

A truly grounded person does not need validation from everyone he or she interacts with to have a positive outlook. It is more of a state of mind and how we see the world. Grounded people allow ourselves to experience sadness, healthy fear, or disappointment, as we understand the flow of life and know that our challenges don't define us. When we feel we're in balance, we're in touch with ourselves and let our intuition guide us. It means we're beginning to fix the mess we may find ourselves in. There are many paths up a mountain—which one is healthy for you?

YOU DON'T HAVE TO BE SEDUCED BY YOUR DARKNESS AND SUFFERING

Our mindset plays a great role in how our life actualizes. We don't always have to be seduced by suffering or darkness. It can be addictive, but we can also imagine how, sometimes, positive things can happen in the down times that bring in darkness. We can also become aware of how, in moments of despair, positive things can occur—kindness from strangers, friends, family. Never forget that at the end of every night, the sun always rises in the morning, no matter what happened at night.

In the same way that we may have learned to tolerate pain, we can teach ourselves to experience lightness. Have you ever had a painful muscle cramp? You may have thought the pain would last forever. It didn't. At some point, the pain dissipated. You can deal with your darkness in a similar way. Instead of trying to navigate around dark patches when they pop up in life, you have been conditioned to either prevent them from emerging altogether or ignoring that they exist. So many try to push these dark moments aside, or, even worse, take medication to suppress them. It is too easy to find someone to write a prescription for a pill to pop. All it does is numb you even more. As much as you may want to believe in medication and the healthcare system, the infrastructure of such doesn't support the philosophy of medical professionals taking the appropriate amount of time to get to know you and your lifestyle enough to truly understand what is best for you. Rather, all this current system supports is shuffling patients in like cattle and churning them out with prescriptions in hand.

You can put the human soul back into the center of life. The only true way you can move forward is to be courageous enough to step into your darkness and be willing to do your work to see where it comes from. In nature, there is a very bright ball of light called the sun that lights the Earth and shines on the darkness to provide the life that sustains us all. The cycles and seasons of life are very powerful, and it is time to accept them as our navigation systems. During the winter, it is time to hide out and tap into our imaginations, dreams, and plans. We emerge in spring to plant seeds and dream. When summer rolls around, it is time to water the seeds and cultivate them. The fall is a time to celebrate the harvest and reap the rewards of our labors. When we are clear on our purpose, we can follow the seasons of life without having to rush from activity to activity. Nature is our biggest teacher and shows us the way from our darkness to our lightness and back again.

Our mental and spiritual strengths are useful tools when facing new obstacles. Whatever challenging story we're facing, there is always someone going through his or her own hell. We can mentally prepare ourselves to jump into the swamp with the alligators when we know that our intention is for the highest good of all and we believe in it wholeheartedly. We can never give up. The biggest challenge can bring upon the biggest success when we nurture ourselves.

Despite setbacks and other various interferences, do your best to stay focused on your purpose and its impact on the lives of others. It is so important to let your purpose fuel you when you get railroaded by the process, or when the system tries to rein you in. It is challenging you to be even more present in the details and to live every moment to the fullest—even during the difficult times. Commit and ride the wave, knowing things can change very quickly and shift for the good at any moment.

It took a lot of unlearning until I learned to be grateful for the times life threw me curve balls, as it always brought important lessons, too. The more I am willing to face situations or traumas in my life, the more I heal. The more I ignore them, the more they come back, again and again, until I face them head on. They require me to find a strong sense of compassion and awareness. I see them as storms entering my life, knowing that sometimes they will tear me apart— but at the end of the day, when I do my work of becoming aware of the lessons I am learning, the storm subsides, and calm prevails. As author Shannon L. Alder said, "Storms don't come to teach us painful lessons, rather they were meant to wash us clean."

The reason we each need to purge, cleanse, and purify ourselves is to make space. By evicting any voice in our mind that feeds our unhealthy limiting beliefs, we open up precious space. We don't need to live in a false sense of happiness any longer. Our opportunity is to come back to balance and know that it's okay to feel deeply about any sadness, anger, or defeat over past events that traumatized us. When we stifle emotions, we go out of balance. When we're ready to face ourselves, we can find harmony again. What I learned is to experiment and start with where I was and become aware of what may be haunting me, and why.

We each face situations in life when things get complicated. Instead of falling into the drama, we can learn to pause ourselves. This is when we can start assessing the situation, ask ourselves questions, and neutralize the panic or anxiety that emerges. It allows us to defuse the intensity of the emotions of the situation and see what is truly happening. What or who is the root cause of your discomfort? Where is the fire? What feelings are being projected to fuel it? What is your role in it, and are you contributing to fanning the flames? Are you willing to change so the fire can die down, and a calm and thought-provoking conversation can take place?

Sometimes it is necessary to get up and walk around, to shift the tension and look for a different perspective. Moving to another area helps to gain an alternative point of view. Like a director dissecting a scene, you can examine all the angles closely from the various cast roles. If you are able to do that, you detach yourself from the emotional attachment and the potential drama unfolding. It doesn't help to become numb and uninvolved—but it does help to look at the situation in an objective way to get a greater understanding of how you want to approach it.

You can experience a high degree of turbulence as pressure mounts in life, but at a certain point, it will release, and you will get to sit back and reflect on what you have learned and created. Sometimes your biggest challenge can turn into your biggest opportunity. Just like a bottle of champagne, the more it is shaken, the more pressure builds up inside. When you eventually uncork it, the cork will fly across the room and the champagne will explode and the bubbles will spill over.

The body, mind, and emotion are what makes us human. Everything begins in the mind, which is our inner life, and is composed of thoughts that inform the heart. We don't always have a lot of choice about the thoughts that appear in our minds, but like an adventurer, we do have the ability to navigate what stays in there and what we let enter our hearts. The heart helps us determine what is ethical and keeps us balanced. The filtering takes place in the liver and the kidneys. Our minds and hearts send messages to our bodies. You achieve mastery when the mind navigates the heart, which then speaks to the body. We're in the process of building bridges so we can be whole and understand our system of thinking. We can become holistic in every aspect of the journey.

ALIGNING WITH THE ELEMENTS TO PURIFY AND CLEANSE

The ground beneath us is literally shifting, and some things may seem out of control as the planet resets. When we're able to purge and cleanse, we learn to call upon compassion to recharge our bodies, minds, and souls. The world is changing and so can each of us. A whole new way of being alive on the planet is emerging and being in the flow is important.

The four elements—earth, air, fire, and water—are integral forces that sustain life. Each element is responsible for different structures in the body. Earth forms solid structures, such as bones, flesh, skin, tissues, and hair. Air is responsible for all movement, including expansion, contraction, and suppression. Water forms saliva, urine, semen, blood, and sweat. Fire forms hunger, thirst, and sleep. When an element is impure or out of balance with another, disease and suffering may occur. There are ways to purify these elements and restore balance and health, and unfold the inner powers and abilities contained in each element through body work—massage, reiki, yoga, tai chi, meditation, exercise, breath work, and a host of other practices.

It's important to become aware of where you get your sense of power and self-esteem. For example, when Earth is out of balance, we're either nurturing everyone else and forgetting about ourselves, or we're being needy and absorbing everyone else's energy. But when earth is balanced, it's the most beautiful expression of nurturing and unconditional love. A lot of us are trying to work through our own self-love.

It is important to stay grounded and connected to the Earth by spending time in nature, walking barefoot in the sand or grass, watching and listening to birds, and all that connects us to what nature shares. The Earth has a natural cleaning power and symbolizes dependability, fertility, stability, orderliness, groundedness, sustenance, prosperity, creativity, physical abundance, nourishment, security, permanence, intuition, introspection, and wisdom. Do you feel connected to the energy of the Earth? Are you aware of how it's changing? Do you feel supported as these changes happen?

Air is connected to the breath of life and all the elements and is the most powerful for cleansing the body of toxins. It fans the fire in our bodies and minds and serves as our life force. Learning how to consciously breathe is a practice that increases inner power. You can find resources online, like Breathe Lab, the brainchild of former Olympic athlete, Tara Sheahan, at http://breathelab.com/. Air symbolizes communication, intelligence, knowledge, perception, learning, thinking, imagination, harmony, movement, and travel. This life source can also, at times, transform into a force of destruction.

Air is the catalyst for change and teaches us to be present. Are you clinging to the past? How can you embrace where you are right now in this present moment?

Fire has transformational and purifying powers as a cleanser, burning up impurities. Fire represents light, and its flame burns through the sun. It can give warmth and enable life, and it can also burn and destroy. Fire symbolizes incredible energy, activity, creativity, passion, freedom, power, love, vision, anger, strength, will, assertiveness, and courage. It can help you to transmute fear that you may be carrying in your body. How do you honor the fire within you?

Water has pure cleansing power. It is symbolic of dreaming, healing, flowing, fluidity, purification, regeneration, stability, strength, change, fertility, devotion, receiving, and unconditional love. Water also symbolizes death, as well as rebirth. It is life-giving but can also be destructive. Fresh water represents a healthy life, while polluted and stagnant water is symbolic of poor health. You can connect with water by connecting your breath to the rhythm of the ocean's waves breaking on the shore. You can also spend time at a river or lake and practice aligning your energy to their natural flow. When a body of water flows unencumbered, it serves as a life force for others—animals, plants, and humans. Do you experience fluidity and flow in your body, or are you filled with toxic thoughts and negative emotions?

Nature continually shows us that everything is interconnected, which is foundational to trekking into the unknown. We don't have to cling to the past when we can embrace who we are right now. While decluttering our homes of unnecessary material items is important, it's also healthy for us to lighten our mental and emotional load and tap into our curiosity and courage as an adventurer on the journey of a lifetime.

CAN YOU MAKE SPACE?

The future path for us as a collective is one of partnership and collaboration to create balance and unity around a shared purpose. To fill the vacuum and replenish what is missing in the world today, we need to be able to create greater balance and unity—to go out into the world and do things as a pioneering leader and creator. By paying closer attention to our thoughts and consciously seeing the connections between our mind, heart, and body, we can become more sensitive and aware. Understanding how we function as individuals and what happens when we come together is a skill. How many of us can bring our individual purpose to mesh with the purposes of others? That is a key question conscious leaders and pioneers in our world are exploring and have explored for centuries.

There are certain aspects, like our DNA that we're born with, that cannot be changed Every single person has his or her own signature that is unique and valuable and specific in character. In essence, you are who you are, and you can do the things you can do. For example, if you are born short, you are short. You can dream about being tall, but the reality is that you are short. So, isn't it simpler to accept who you are? Try to find the value within your own DNA that you received. There are people of all varying heights and weights all over the world, each bringing their own unique value in their own special way, regardless of their body structure and looks.

You really do have everything inside of you, and there is no need to continue to look for answers outside of yourself. If more people find a way to learn to respect and see our own value, peace would prevail. It is so easy to lose our connection to our own value. When we have brown eyes, we may dream of having blue eyes. When we have black hair, we may wish we were blond. If we're losing our hair and going bald, we probably dream of a full head of hair. For some reason, the emphasis on creating inner harmony and full acceptance of self is often missing and is a vital piece of our self-worth when stepping out into the world.

Inner balance comes when we are comfortable with the gifts and talents we have been given. We have yet to be able to import changes to our DNA. Anything we try to change artificially is not really authentic. When humans mess around with nature, it seems we always pay the price. When we bring forth artificial solutions that are unnatural, there are always consequences. As neuroscientist and shamanic healer, Dr. Natalie Leigh Dyer, reminds us, "Stillness is a requirement to know who we truly are. The many distractions of the world have seduced us into unconsciousness. However, we choose to distract ourselves. Allow yourself the stillness to experience the ever-present higher self, the watcher of the little you. This must be done in the Now. Calm the mind, the conditioned thought chatter, breathe fully, and just BE for a moment each day."

Balance occurs when all of the natural ingredients of life fit together. You may be seeking stability and comfort in conformity. If you are not finding it and are in constant search mode, maybe it is time to explore another route. As Homer expressed in *The Odyssey*, "You have to lose yourself to find yourself," so don't give up on your search, but be prepared to dig out your true self from the rubble and not leave your truth buried forever. Is it time to dig into your adventurous side and explore what's possible?

EXPEDITION 15

WHAT'S YOUR ENOUGH?

A
t some point in my life, I had enough and I couldn't take it anymore. One of my breaking points came when I won a coveted award from a well-respected Silicon Valley organization and came home and cried. Imagine that you were at a gala to receive an award with five other leaders in the industry, each also known as a "winner." You are lined up in a row and it is your turn to step on the stage and accept this honor in front of a very large crowd. But, suddenly, you are physically pushed aside by one of the other recipients who races to the stage. She is about to climb the stairs with a huge smile on her face, when your picture is projected on the screens and you are invited to the stage. Can you imagine how you would feel at that moment?

I stood there, quite shocked, as they called out my name and watched this award winner who—instead of climbing the steps to accept the award—stepped away when she realized it was not her turn. This woman's smile disappeared, and a state of confusion formed on her face. The only story I could tell myself was that she must have been so nervous that something grabbed her to be hypnotized by the winner's circle. But it was now my so-called moment and spotlight. What the people in the audience did not know was that in a few seconds, some big shifts happened inside of me. I realized the outside world could not bring me recognition and validation because this was not the world, I wanted to live in. This award lost its meaning in one moment. And instead of thanking people for the award, I openly shared some of my thoughts on compassion and truly seeing each other. I went home to reflect on why being recognized by my "community" made me feel so utterly empty when so many people dream of receiving the award.

What I didn't tell you is that right before they lined us up to go on stage, I saw the leader of this organization push and bully one of the wait staff out of the corner of my eye. My friends had to stop me from getting involved by reminding me that this was my moment. I sat there, shocked, and told them that we had to leave and that I could not accept an award from an organization whose executive director acted this way. My friend, Amy, who knows me well, tried to calm me down and told me I deserved the recognition that night and we could deal with the situation later. And thirty seconds later, I was called to line up for the stage and almost got trampled. It was a night to remember what life is truly about. I learned that I didn't want to live in a world that gives out awards only celebrating those who are considered the best—just because we've jumped through all of the right hoops, and not much more. It creates so much unnecessary angst and a fake reality. I just wanted to do my best—but not at the expense of myself or anyone else. Staying in that story was not my answer or way of life—creating a healthier one was.

ARE YOU ENOUGH?

I found myself asking the age-old question: when is enough, enough? And more importantly, a new question emerged, which was, "What *is* my enough?" When have we had enough fear, worry, or joy? How much stuff do we need? At what point have we consumed enough of the best life, the best food, the best friends? How many countries do we need to visit to feel satisfied? How many people need to validate us? How many successes do we need? How many items should be on our bucket list? And when can we let go of the stories that keep us stuck? When is enough truly *enough*?

The story goes that writers Kurt Vonnegut, best known for his bestselling novel, *Slaughterhouse Five,* and Joseph Heller, author of *Catch-22,* were guests at a party in the expansive second home of their billionaire host. Vonnegut described the exchange in an article published in the *New Yorker* in 2005:

"I said, 'Joe, how does it make you feel to know that our host only yesterday may have made more money than your novel, *Catch-22,* has earned in its entire history?' And Joe said, 'I've got something he can never have.' And I said, 'What on earth could that be, Joe?' And Joe said, 'The knowledge that I've got enough.'"

Vonnegut crystallized the crux of our predicament in which he distilled the secret of happiness into the knowledge that *"[you've] got enough—a knowledge that seems to only grow exponentially more elusive as our civilizational clock continues ticking."*

What I discovered is that our *enough* largely depends on whether we want to live in the material world, which is disconnected and monetizes nature, or whether we want to experience life on our own terms. Our mind has been programmed to tell us one thing or the other: what we don't have, what we think we need, why this isn't good, and why that isn't enough. Perhaps the only certainty we have is *uncertainty*. When we learn to live with unpredictability and uncertainty, we can begin to learn how to increasingly become resilient and develop our ability to recover from setbacks—because we can be certain that they will continue to pop up on our path. We can choose the material items that truly bring value into our lives, so we don't have to stuff ourselves with things that have no true meaning.

Have you ever watched trees during a storm? If you have, you know how fascinating it is to see how they dance with the wind. But to do so, the trees must be grounded with strong roots and a high degree of flexibility to withstand the gusts of winds that will come their way. The trees also need the intelligence of an underground community of trees—plants and fungi to support them. A tree does not need to win an award for being the best tree to withstand a storm, but it does need to do its best. Nature is our teacher and shows us that to survive a storm, knowing what our *enough* is helps us let go of outdated beliefs we carry, as well as habitual reactions as to how to respond.

Being grounded in reality, like the trees, helps us understand the need for inner stability. Our inner guide helps us stay grounded when unexpected storms arrive in life. When we're not grounded, we tend to live in fear or panic, and react to any change with stress and increasing burnout. We may find ourselves wallowing in thoughts like, "Why does this happen to me?" Our opportunity is to not stay stuck in unhealthy patterns, but to see the opportunity the storm brings and gain perspective on how we can respond in a healthy way.

Renowned Mycologist (a person who studies fungi), Paul Stamets, believes that, "[The] mycelium network represents rebirth, rejuvenation, regeneration. Fungi generate soil that gives life. The task that we face today is to understand the language of Nature. My mission is to discover the language of the fungal networks that communicate with the ecosystem. And I for one believe that Nature is intelligent . . . and if we don't get our act together and come in commonality and understanding with the organisms that sustain us today, not only will we destroy those organisms, but we will destroy ourselves. We need to have a paradigm shift in our consciousness. What will it take to achieve that? If I die trying but I'm inadequate to the task to make a course change in the evolution of this planet, the fact is that I tried. How many people are not trying? If you knew that every breath you took could save hundreds of lives into the future had you walked down this path of knowledge, would you run down this path of knowledge as fast as you could?"

The key is to be rooted in the ground and understand our connection to the soil and earth. The underground network beneath our feet is made of fungi and called the mycelial network. By linking to the fungal network, plants and trees help their neighbors by sharing nutrients and information—or sabotage unwelcome plants by spreading toxic chemicals through the "Wood Wide Web." Native Americans had a planting technique called the "Three Sisters," where they would plant corn, bean, and squash crops close to each other. The corn provides a structure for the beans to climb, the beans give nitrogen to the soil, and the squash spreads on the ground to prevent weeds from growing.

There is much intelligence under our feet. And because we have been disconnected from the intelligence of nature, we have simply lost our way. Nature is somewhere we are told to go to detox or get some fresh air, but when you actually tap into the intelligence beneath your feet, you will be reminded that you are simply part of it. It is not a place that is apart from you. The mycelial network can show you how to self-organize and coexist in a community. If you were fungi, you would naturally build a whole connected network. You would not have barriers to self-organizing and would find a way to connect.

The fungal internet exemplifies one of the great lessons of ecology: seemingly separate organisms are often interconnected and may depend on each other. The Wood Wide Web seems to be a crucial part of how these connections form. Like the trees, knowing your *enough* will come from us working together, even with people we don't always agree with, to create healthy systems. Like the world under your feet with its natural intelligence, it will come from our collective intelligence of knowing when enough is enough so we can set aside our deep divisions and unite with kindness and shared purpose.

When I moved to California, I started to garden for the first time in my life. I loved persimmons and planted a tree, along with a fig, loquat, and apple trees. Every year, I would see the flowers blossom but there would be no persimmons. And then, on its ninth year—the year I sold my house and left—the permissions appeared in abundance. Nature does not rush as it follows its cycles. I realized that I planted the trees so others can enjoy their fruits. I learned to embrace and welcome every moment of my enough as I put down the manual and followed my heart.

When you become more forgiving and trusting of yourself, and then others, you can then see with new eyes what your *enough* truly is. You will stop the need to fight and to win and understand that it's your time to simply create with meaning and abundant inner wisdom. And then you can celebrate all that you are without needing anyone else's stamp of approval. When you live in your truth, you will no longer need someone else's award to validate you—but you may have found some other deep lesson that brought you to this same place I found myself.

WHAT'S YOUR STORY?

Our world needs people who know how to build trust-filled relationships. People who know how to collaborate, cooperate, and support a functional community. We need these people more than we need celebrities or heroes who "inspire" us to be like them. Should your inspiration not come from you? There is an illusion that fame and money will lead us to the magical door of luxury and happiness. Yet, the more time we spend with people who have attained these levels of societal success, the more we realize they are really ordinary people who gained an audience and are handsomely paid for their work. Actors, for example, take on roles to entertain us and bring stories—drama, tragedy, horror, mystery, thriller, comedy—into our life. However, there is an artificial allure that they have the successful life we want. This is the path they took and their life isn't better than anyone else's, as they have their own issues and wounds to deal with that fame and money can't heal. You have your own life, your own canvas, and your own ability to seek your true intentions. When we continually consume the onslaught of external noise, we will never find our own truth, as it is not in anyone else's story but our own.

When celebrities or billionaires announce they are supporting a charitable cause with a donation of millions or billions of dollars, do we ever stop and think that it is our money that they are donating? Where does their affluence come from, and why do we continue to celebrate them and give them our endorsements through our consumption? And what about kids who want to be heroes just like them, so they can acquire the same level of societal admiration?

The healthy psyche feels itself to be on a journey, but most people are still waiting for a strong leader or some sort of sign to marshal us forward. There is the recurring mythology of the lone cowboy riding into town and leading everyone to nirvana by saving everyone or standing up to a vengeful bully. There is a belief that someone better will step up and show us the way. And thus, power is given away to an external belief over and over. But you can decide to turn your back on being dominated by the past and prevent the repetition of unhealthy versions of old cycles by understanding your *enough*. Leadership is not outside yourself.

Too often, you are told that your story needs to be one of the heroes, where you dominate nature and are celebrated for being innovative, competitive, and a ruthless winner in life. The mythology of the hero and the associated archetypes are provided in abundance, as the story you were told was that to be the best and get to the top, you must step on others to win the award, the title, and the respect you are owed. But what if this has never been your story?

When you are willing to look close enough, you will start witnessing the world around you, especially when you start doing your own exploration and research. Many of us no longer want to live a life of division and spend our precious time in antiquated win-lose scenarios in pursuit of being the hero. What do you actually win at the end of the day? Our natural inclination is to crave meaningful collaboration, cooperation, dialogue, and interconnectedness—but we simply forgot how to show up with integrity to pursue co-creation and build community effortlessly. This is what is possible when you open your mind and heart to seeing that there is another way. But it takes work to unravel what has been created and step forward to create a healthy path where we can lift each other up, as there is no need to live in a divided world of heroes and villains.

Think about what story you would like to be part of creating in the future when you read this one. For a number of generations now, parents wanted to give their children what they didn't have—whether it was an education or greater opportunity, as well as material items from toys, better house, car, and electronics. When parents buy stuff, children are happy. But only for a short time, since they get addicted to the culture of *more is better* with never-ending new and improved products promoted by corporations that are only too thrilled for us to consume.

A survey of young adults found that 81 percent believe the most important goal of their generation is to "become rich." It is how they have been conditioned to define being a successful human being. And yet, all the research in the world has shown that people who focus on material gain have high rates of physical and mental challenges and stay stuck in the never-ending pursuit of money and fame. Business, especially advertisers, are only too happy to fuel these beliefs and then offer credit cards and debt to fund messages like "you deserve the best" and "more is better." The truth is that these organizations' success depends on how many people adopt their messages and consume more and more material items—their growth and life depend on it. And who doesn't want to have the latest and greatest?

It is only when parents examine their own attitude toward money and fame, and the impact of what they are teaching their children through their own behavior, that change can happen. So many people today call out technology and social media as evil, and yet we're the ones who created these technologies and platforms. Who are we blaming, and why are we even blaming the technology? Maybe, instead of blaming, we can take a step back and look at this problem with an opportunity mindset of finding the value in these creations.

Today, many people complain about the fact that kids bring their mobile devices to the dinner table and interact with them during mealtime. When I was a kid, my parents did not allow us to come to any meals until we were fully dressed in what they considered proper. There were no pajamas allowed. While education was very important to both my parents, and they passed on their love of books, we were never allowed to read at the table. Mealtime at our house was about conversation and dialogue. We were not allowed to watch television or do anything that would disrupt our family time. It was simple, and it helped me develop a yearning for amazing dinner gatherings when I was older, where mealtime was considered sacred.

Can we remember what the purpose of mealtime is and make it about connecting around healthy food and conversation? The opportunity is not to throw more material stuff at the problem, but to find opportunities to connect deeply with our children and spend quality time creating together. This is foundational to being a conscious leader of your life—being able to reevaluate, question, and become aware that there is a healthier way. When was the last time you had healthy dialogue? What made it memorable?

Conscious leadership in our life is not about staying stuck in blaming a force outside yourself—be it technology or consumerism—but rather about what is unhealthy in the world. It is about knowing that as a parent, family member, friend, or citizen of the world, you may want to create a healthier world for yourself. As a young person, you are left wondering what leadership actually means and questioning what makes a great leader. The answer lies in finding the leader in yourself who wants to step out and create something meaningful (to you) in the world, and connect with others who share your vision and drive to action.

So, when is enough *enough*? And what is your *enough*? This is a foundational question to help guide us. Human history, as well as our own, will repeat itself until we become aware of the patterns. And we can see only when we're ready to unravel our conditioning—and not everyone is ready to do our deep inner work. So many people today are calling out fake news, fake gurus, and fake love. It is much easier to point fingers and blame the other. It is much more challenging to take accountability and become aware of our role within the story, and even history. The opportunity is right here, staring us in the face. It has always been here. We just forgot. We may seek time in nature, when we are a part of it. And even if we live in a big city, almost everything we have that has not been genetically modified comes from nature. Someone with curiosity and imagination created something useful for us to enjoy during our precious time here on Earth.

This is an amazing time to be alive, and when we can turn down the volume on the noise of the world, we will see the patterns we have collectively created and understand that history does not need to repeat itself. You can say *enough* and do your part without slinging mud, or you can watch history lather, rinse, lather, repeat. Author and Professor Maxine Hong Kingston writes, "In a time of destruction, create something. A poem. A parade. A community. A school. A vow. A moral principle. One peaceful moment."

We live in amazing times—but they can also be overwhelming, as there is so much information out there to discern. Some of our food and products come with warning labels, informing us they are toxic and hazardous for our health. Someone made that decision for us as to when to be careful, and they don't always have our wellbeing in mind. But people, ideas, beliefs, and news do not come with any warning labels. There are people and organizations who want to get our attention and validation; it makes them stronger when we buy into them, especially when they are narcissistic or toxic.

Your feelings of being or having enough matter, as it is an opportunity to tap into your inner knowing of what is healthy and unhealthy for you. The way you respond to everything in your environment has an impact. The world you live in offers you abundant opportunities to go down as many rabbit holes as you choose. You can literally spend your days online, and in front of different media, absorbing information from a multitude of sources. You don't have to search far for the problems that surround you in this world; they can appear in a flash and take you on a ride of anger, despair, shame, judgement, and blame. Do you know what actually happens to you when you take this ride? It takes you into a negative state of mind that siphons your energy and distracts you from what really matters: your personal freedom to know how you want to show up in the world and co-create what is possible. What happens when you observe where you get stuck and whether the stories around your *enough* are truly yours or someone else's?

A lot can happen when you question your *enough*. As Albert Einstein wrote in "My Credo" in 1932, "Although I am a typical loner in my daily life, my awareness of belonging to the invisible community of those who strive for truth, beauty, and justice has prevented me from feelings of isolation." When you are aware of your *enough*, you are never truly alone.

WHAT IF YOU SHIFTED YOUR FOCUS TO THE MOST PRECIOUS RESOURCE YOU HAVE?

And no, it's not money. Some say money is like air—an abundant resource that is always available. Money comes and money goes, and it's the choices we make about how much we think we need, how much we spend, and what we consume. No matter how much money we have or think we need, the only thing money can't buy is time and health. Imagine a world where we respected our time as much as we did money. Time is so precious that every year we celebrate our birthdays by giving and receiving gifts. But as we get older, there is a generation of people who are starting to value experiences more than gifts. We have been numbing ourselves with stuff as a way to compensate ourselves with the latest trendy clothing, accessories, gadgets, or whatever we think will make us happy. But more and more, people are finding that we want to declutter our lives so we can fully experience them. Simplicity is becoming more appealing as a way of life.

Attachment to anything or anyone causes us to obsess or worry about it, and this is true when it comes to our *enough* with the flow of money in our life. An Achuar tribesman shared that when he first left the Amazon Rainforest to visit the West, he was astounded by the concept of money. He couldn't just pick fruit off trees on the streets of a city, hunt, or drink clean water whenever he needed to. Everything he needed to consume required him to have money to buy it, when back in the forest, he could hunt and gather what was abundant with others.

We are the ones who created money and the stock market, and decided which natural resources were expensive (gold) and which were cheap (sand). The only thing that does not cost money is the air we consume. And we don't experience the same attachment to air as we do to money. This tribesman was actually shocked to see the carelessness and pollution of air everywhere he visited, knowing that every breath we take is dependent on air. Imagine for a moment that you were this Achuar man and it was your first time leaving the comfort of the Amazon Rainforest to experience the other world. What would you experience in his shoes? What would you observe and become aware of from his perspective?

When you live your life for money, prestige, or approval, you most likely are not getting up every day thrilled to start your day and full of gratitude when it's time to go to bed at night. And when you try to live your life in certainty and predictability in an uncertain world, you often stop yourself from going inside and finding out what it is you truly want to create. Some of the simplest things in life can often give you much deeper rewards than materialistic ones. You got the fancy car, became a bestselling author, won the championship, or whatever it is that provides the status you thought you wanted—but now what? And when you don't win any of these, why do you often find yourself feeling like a loser? Who has the power to put you in this box?

WHICH MINDSET ARE YOU CHOOSING?

Isn't it ironic that we live in a world of abundance and yet scarcity programming has been planted in so many minds? When you perceive that something is scarce, you most likely become obsessed by that thing. Most of us have been immersed in a scarcity belief system, which has created habits deeply rooted in the belief that there is not enough—and *you* are not enough. Many have become addicted to busyness, as we believe the scarcity of time forces us to hurry and check everything off our never-ending lists.

Money has turned into a lifeline that is valued in certain parts of the world more than natural resources, like access to clean air and water. The belief in the scarcity of money has created an industry of greed where habits like being the best are rewarded and celebrated. But from the scarcity of meaningful work comes burnout, anxiety, and depression. These are modern day afflictions that are not openly discussed, leaving us unsure as to how to shift this unhealthy belief system.

When you know your *enough* about money and you are not obsessing about it, you have to decide whether having stuff like the latest Lamborghini would truly make you happy after the fleeting months of excitement. One day, you may find someone keyed the door of your new car and you feel angry over how it is no longer perfect and find yourself fretting over who would commit such a destructive crime against another. And yes, it is horrible, but we also do not live in a perfect world. Most people may pretend to be happy for you, but jealousy and envy run in the minds of many people. It is a non-stop race to the top of being celebrated for standing out in some way. But at the end of the day, what matters most to you? Do you know what *your* enough is to live *your* healthy life?

The only certainty you have in life is that one day you will die.

It's only a question of when. There is nothing else in your life that is as certain as death. And until you come face to face with its reality, you live your life according to the big plan, whatever you choose it to be. So why do you worry more about money than how you spend the precious time you have? According to Lynne Swift in *The Soul of Money*, "When you let go of trying to get more of what you don't really need, it frees up oceans of energy to make a difference with what you have."

Think about this one question: "What is my *enough*?" Take a moment to jot down what comes to you when it comes to relationships or partnerships in your life, how many have you been led to believe you need? And how many are truly enough for you? What are the most valuable relationships in your life that nourish you? What about your work, how you spend your time, and how much money you really need to live a full life the way you want to? What is it that you need to help you live a healthy life? And when is enough really enough?

When you realize what your *enough* is, instead of pursuing someone else's purpose or dream, you will let out a big sigh. When you realize the people who are judging you don't actually have their shit together, you will laugh or cry. You will realize that you get to write the rules for how you want to spend your time and life. If you are lucky enough to know how to make the changes necessary to achieve a simpler life defined by your *enough*, you will use time as a way to make important choices—how you get to work, live, and play.

Knowing your *enough* comes from understanding that there is nothing lacking and there are abundant opportunities and possibilities. Ask yourself, is more truly better? When you embrace your *enough*, you'll be rich in so many ways. You won't be rushing or addicted to achieving it all. What could possibly be more important than your wellbeing and your sanity, from which all else springs?

According to author Toni Morrison, "At some point in life the world's beauty becomes enough. You don't need to photograph, paint, or even remember it. It is enough." What is it that you need to live your life's meaning fully? I bet when you truly invest the time in yourself to answer this question and use your own metrics as you define success, you will make healthier choices about who you spend time with and what's truly important in your life. The gift will be that you will know how to stop numbing yourself with things that only money can buy and spend your time living fully. "It is hard work and great art to make life not so serious," wrote author John Irving. How seriously are you taking life?

EXPEDITION 16

I KNOW WHY THE CAGED BIRD SINGS

he poet Maya Angelou, in her book, *I Know Why the Caged Bird Sings,* provides many insights, including this one:

"The caged bird sings with a fearful trill,
of things unknown, but longed for still,
and his tune is heard on the distant hill,
for the caged bird sings of freedom."

Candy stores are filled with abundant sweets. Sugar is not the healthiest choice for our wellbeing—it only gives a temporary high and we will crash until our next "fix." When we have a sweet tooth, we crave more sugar—it's a form of addiction. Each of us can imprison ourselves in stories that do not have any physical bars, like needing the sugar high that is unhealthy for us. When we are unaware of our obsessions, they can lead us to another prison sentence when our health deteriorates from the overload. Most of our life is spent telling ourselves stories and listening to those of others about what we must have and who we must be. Society recognizes us according to what we have and what we own. We can unconsciously self-sentence ourselves into a life without parole.

Modern society sometimes has a fast track to depreciate our dreams into a harsh reality. Activist Jasmine Burnett believes that, "A tornado comes with a vengeance, but its vengeance is not against you; it's against the things that hurt you and keep you disconnected from your purpose. We're the tornado. A tornado creates conditions for the impossible. It doesn't wait for you to recognize your liberation. The aggressive, unyielding love of the tornado doesn't allow you to run away from yourself."

Society has taught us to find shelter, which serves as our foundational structure and security from exposure to the elements. We're also faced with a myriad of choices, like who we work for, how we live, what we own, who we marry, and whether or not we bring children into the world. And once we make our choices, some may feel joyful while others feel resentful and trapped in a cage. We can choose to stay married or leave. But what matters most is to be honest with ourselves. Many stay because it's honorable to be responsible and not disappoint our elders, and we may convince ourselves that that's our only option. But there's no safety when the foundation of our shelter is rotting.

I've been in many situations, as I'm sure you have, where I knew my life would completely change if I walked out the door into the unknown. But no matter how hard it was, I taught myself to listen to that voice inside of me instead of the one of disappointment of not living up to someone else's expectations. I promised myself that as one door closed, a few windows would open, and I would learn from each experience that made me uncomfortable. I learned to accept people as they are so I can be who I am meant to be.

This work is definitely not for the faint of heart. It's not easy to choose to break free from the expectations that often put us on autopilot as a way to navigate life. It requires many deaths and rebirths—breaking it down and building it up. And one thing that it allows us to choose is whether we live our life in a cage. Life in the cage often feels like everything is falling apart and needs some fixing, which is exhausting and overwhelming. But once we can free ourselves, we can see that nothing needs to be fixed.

In *Build It Up,* American singer-songwriter Ingrid Michaelson sings, "Open up your fist and let me out. I was made to run around and let me feel the air beneath my feet. Let me go. And I know not everybody gets a new life. And I know not everybody gets to start over again. But I do know what I'm doing with my new life. I'll build it up, break it down, build it up. You can fly away too, that's on you. But don't tell me what I cannot do. I can tie on my shoes and put on my coat. I'm living a history, the one that I wrote."

UNSTUFFING OURSELVES

You may have inherited some beliefs of what will give you a better life. Then one day, you wake up and realize you've been misled when you have to face the harsh reality that life has not turned out the way you were promised. You recognize so much of what you have been fed about how your life is supposed to be is merely an illusion.

We all need material items in life—ones that have a purpose and functionality. However, we can remain alert not to worship and be enamored with them in any way. They can enhance life, but they can never bring us more than temporary satisfaction. What purpose do material items play in your life? Are you constantly out there accumulating more and more stuff, or are you taking what you need and enjoying it?

Many of us are numbing and nurturing ourselves with material things and it is easy to see why. Everywhere we turn, someone has a product that claims to make our life better—whether it be the best car, the latest designer jeans, a new espresso machine, instant pot, or the best toothpaste. When a product or service stipulates that it can make our life so much better, the associated subliminal message is that our life is lacking without it. The global advertising revenue is at an all-time high, forecasted to reach $615 billion in 2020. The beauty industry alone is projected at close to $480 billion!

One aspect these figures address is that we worship our body and its appearance—not necessarily its health and wellness. Billions of dollars are spent on beauty products to pursue the perfect look set by the fashion industry and to imitate the beauty of celebrity icons, and now, even a growing industry of reality TV "stars." It has made us addicted to the endless pursuit of perfecting how we look, and completely overlooking how we feel inside. Our spirit often gets left behind in the illusion of perfection as our ego drives our persona. And yet, in wanting to feel truly healthy, it is necessary to unite all the pieces of ourselves to feel whole. Mind, body, and spirit are all one package and it requires our daily attention and investment to all these individual parts, otherwise we get lost in the wrappers.

There is a direct correlation to keeping society consuming unconsciously in a desire to need and want more stuff that makes organizations reach their growth targets. The successful business model is to ensure growth by achieving sales targets and creating healthy profit margins, but there is an even more serious downside to this formula than keeping our bank accounts drained. Our psyche is being fed an underlying assumption that to feel good about ourselves, we need to have the latest, perfect items—whether it is the perfect house, perfect partner, perfect job, perfect car, perfect outfits, perfect friends, or the perfect vacation. What if the answer cannot be found in perfection? What if we each knew what our *enough* is, when it comes to food, friends, money, work, and every aspect of life?

It feels like many of us have stuffed ourselves with more and more to make ourselves feel like we have arrived and are successful. Materialism comes from a place of scarcity and lack—a feeling of not being good enough or not having enough in an abundant and prosperous world of opportunity. Somewhere along the line, someone convinced us that more is better. But where we're headed, all we're being asked to consider is making conscious decisions about what we consume.

There is a growing movement urging humanity to be more mindful of the footprints we're leaving behind and to minimize the negative impact our current lifestyles are making. There is an increasing number of people who are becoming aware of taking only what we need and refusing to define ourselves by our possessions. Exposing ourselves to a plethora of lifestyles and different views, we're able to observe the differences and a growing divide in the world—not just in terms of gender, race, and class, but also to many other groups that society likes to assign labels to.

Wherever and whatever we perceive to be a lack in the world, we are ready and willing to stand up for it and make a difference. Some are making different choices, which can be classified as conscious. This means we are actively making healthy choices, like not buying or working for organizations that make a profit from destroying the Earth and our bodies. Being part of a collective conscious community asks us to consider the effect on our planet and truly understand the role balance, harmony, wholeness, and integration play in our daily lives and the communities we bring together. As Laura Eisenhower, the great-granddaughter of President Dwight David Eisenhower, reminds us, "We are each other. We chose to come in diverse bodies, to unify, not separate. We are truly One and beautifully diverse."

THE UNEXAMINED LIFE

As Socrates is noted for uttering in Plato's Apology, "the unexamined life is not worth living." He attributed these words when faced with execution rather than a commitment to silence or exile. His political association with an earlier regime, the Athenian democracy, charged Socrates with corrupting young people and undermining state religion. Free thinking allows us to uncover the mysteries of life. We come into this world with the ability to make conscious decisions, and to experience the whole gamut of being fully human. Socrates himself demonstrated in his own life (and death) that being fully human can be extremely challenging. In a world of complexity and uncertainty, there exists the allure of others whose opinions and beliefs offer answers, directions, and precise instructions on how to live life. It demands, however, that we set aside any self-examination and merely comply, to toe the line and follow customs and practices. Yet it prevents us from knowing our own truth and experiencing our own beauty and gentleness.

There are ample opportunities to decide on your journey between convenient conventionality and devotion to truth and evolution. It is your choice to determine whether you, like Socrates, deserve to call your life worthy. No one else can. It is also up to you to define the meaning of the life you aspire to experience. It is a path that is open for anyone who can shed societal conformity by purifying, cleansing, and making space for you to evolve. You can, of course, stay where you are if you are feeling safe, but you will have to step out of the old comfortable paradigm of existence if you want something different and unknown. It's always a choice.

Before making any long-term commitments or big decisions, are you aware of any excuses that may be shackling you to your status quo? Can you evaluate how badly you really want something, and whether the need is greater than the consequences? Is it worthwhile to stay where you are, or add it to your futuristic bucket list? There are invisible bars all around you. Become aware of the tug-of-war inside you that asks, "What will happen when I cross that invisible bar—and what happens if I don't?" The more you procrastinate and avoid the dilemma, the more it grows and keeps you imprisoned. Why not invite yourself to have a conversation with your fear of the unknown? What would you say? What would you hear? What would you learn?

It's usually not until we finally cross an invisible bar that we feel we have actually taken a step forward. This bar doesn't become visible until we become fully conscious that it is there—and the reason why it's there in the first place. Become grateful for what you perceive as detours, roadblocks, setbacks, heartbreaks, and abrasive and disappointing people. You will eventually see there was a purpose for these obstacles because they protect you and redirect you from places that were not meant for you to experience. Be conscious of how much energy you give these lessons and tune your dimmer switch accordingly.

THE ART OF CREATION IS AVAILABLE IN EVERY MOMENT

When adding lemon or honey to your iced tea, you will most likely stir it. You can't expect your iced tea to taste the same once these things are combined. You create a new flavor. The elements cannot stay the same and will only produce a new creation like sweet tea. It has to change. When you are on a path to create something new, you cannot focus on the old ingredients that led you to your present moment. You must embrace the mystery that this path is now offering you.

The world is constantly changing, and you have a choice as to whether you go with the flow or stay where you are. Surprisingly, the unknown is far vaster than you could ever imagine, and certainly far greater than what you know. With this knowledge, where would you put your attention and investment?

Imagine if children were taught that it is the journey that matters most and not the destination of achievement. The present is a split second and the past is no longer relevant. The past cannot sustain the present; it has to be built upon. The stories in your mind that tell you can't do certain things can keep you stuck. Past traumas, wounds, or injustices hold you back with a deep fear of the unknown, but the healthiest thing you can ask yourself in these circumstances is, "What's the worst thing that could happen if I take this path or make this choice?" If your answers are along the lines of, "I could fail. I will be embarrassed and humiliated. I could be proven wrong," isn't it time to realize you can survive these feelings? This is a particularly powerful technique when you stumble or hit a roadblock and need to regroup and start again.

THE ART OF LETTING GO

Most of us receive our education through the school system, and yet we're rarely taught practical skills that help us navigate our day-to-day life and empower us to be a productive member of society. There are very few "practical class of life" semesters currently being offered at schools, especially ones tailored to our experiences. When we no longer want to consume someone else's meal plan and uncover our own path, there is the school of life that is ready to accept us at any point. And what you will not easily find in the mainstream news are the parents and teachers who are unschooling their children and creating healthy, holistic ways to raise our future generations. We have more freedom than we ever imagined when we release ourselves from the agendas that are unhealthy for our personal wellbeing. There are abundant online media resources (should you choose to connect with them) working day and night to provide us with alternative information and open conversations, while facing increasing censorship.

Your responsibility is always to ask yourself tough questions and go deep into your soul to find out what you are made of. Regardless of what anyone else may think is cool, hip, and trendy, the real questions are—what makes you tick? How do you want to live your own life? How do you want to contribute to society? How are you unique and different? Why not share your ideas? Be generous, speak up, and shine your light in the world. It is not about being like everyone else and copying their mojo, but finding your own expression and being yourself, whatever is authentic for you.

Life is an amazing adventure, and it offers tremendous landscapes and a huge range of different lifestyles to be explored. There is a great opportunity to interact with a variety of people from different walks of life that affords us to get to know ourselves more deeply through these connections. The more you explore the world, the easier it is to realize that you have more power than you could ever imagine. There is so much joy to gain from going out in the world and creating. The fun is being part of a concept that turns into a reality that benefits others.

There have been beliefs and ideas that have been given to us that are detrimental to our well-being. These have undermined our mindset and are counterproductive towards living a healthy life. Our work, as we become more aware, is to recognize the beliefs we have inherited that are outdated to disentangle, cleanse, and release them. What are some of the distorted ideas or beliefs you have been infected with? Can you name them and slowly step back and observe them? Is it hard for you to even consider that these are harmful, like infections that carry disease and cause pain and suffering?

Some people would say that this is hard and/or impossible. You may be asking yourself, "How could I possibly take on such a difficult, insurmountable task?" My answer is simple. You may have ingrained habits that are hard to recognize and impossible to pinpoint. Try taking a step back and asking yourself another question: "How do I define *easy* or *hard*? How do I know if it's hard or easy without taking on the task and finding out for myself?"

This is the part that keeps many people stuck in the status quo. You may have convinced yourself how something will play out before you even try it. When you keep telling yourself the same story, you continue to produce the same story. When you want something you've never had, you have to do something you've never done.

Sure, it may be hard for you. Only you know whether it is or not. All we're questioning is, how do you know the outcome when you haven't even started?

BREAKING OUT OF NORMAL WITH MINDFUL MEDICINE

Imagine an orchard with twenty-eight trees, and you were told there is only one that is bearing fruit and brimming with delicious apples. Almost everyone would head to that one tree and fight for his or her fair share of the crop. Why? We've been raised in a herd mentality and trained to follow the leader because we've been repeatedly told he or she knows what's best for us. There will be a few that will break from the herd to discover their own tree and seek out other opportunities to enjoy. Our curiosity will naturally compel us to wander alone and explore. Yet, ironically, many are wanting to experience the best that life has to offer and somehow end up fighting over scarce resources when, in actuality, there is a whole orchard available for us to play in and explore. But we can't until we purge and cleanse ourselves internally as much as externally.

What is needed today is mindful medicine—medicine for our souls—and it does not come in a capsule or a pill. The biggest shift humanity is in need of is a healthy, holistic mindset. Our collective and individual thinking has been infected with unhealthy beliefs that are harmful and poisonous. They are growing like weeds in our systems and bringing disease and illness that is weakening—not strengthening—our foundation and infrastructure.

There is a growing body of research that shows that a healthy diet—high in vegetables and fruits, whole grains, healthy fats, and full of minerals—can prevent depression. And an unhealthy diet—high in processed and genetically modified foods—increases the risk of disease. The daily choices you make matter. You may feel it is too expensive to eat healthy, and that is your reality, but are you aware of whether you are letting toxic people or thoughts into your soul? The Divine did not create stress; humans constructed it and let it in on their own.

Now . . . take as much time as you need to reflect on these questions for the soul medicine that would work for you—free, without a prescription or side effects. Ask yourself any or all of these questions and add some of your own that are sitting deep inside, waiting for the opportunity to emerge.

- In our hearts, we know it is the quality of life that matters most and nurtures us. Are you conscious of the thoughts that are feeding your mind, the food that is nourishing your body, the people close to your heart, and the beliefs fueling your spirit? Can you identify where your stress comes from? And what about joy? What role does it play in your life?

- The biggest journey we're on has always been one of self-discovery. Have you found your voice in how you're expressing yourself? Do you feel caged in, or free to be you?

- You control the volume of the noise and harmony in your world. What and who gets your attention? When you're consuming other people's opinions, diets, menus, beliefs, and thoughts that are not your own, whose are they? What charges you and what drains you?

CHOOSING TO LIVE IN A WORLD OF PERCEIVED CERTAINTY OR UNCERTAINTY

When healthy conditions are in place, you can grow enough crops—fruits, vegetables, and grains—necessary to sustain yourself. There is no need to crowd around one tree when there are plenty of others—and when you can even decide to plant more trees! When you adopt a healthy mindset, there is always another way or solution to be found. Every living being has a different function and purpose. Nature demonstrates this all the time. There are beautiful flowers to invite the bees to pollinate and produce honey, fruit and nut trees to nourish us and the animals, and to provide shade. Even poison ivy, while feared by humans, is food for bears and deer.

Can we end the endless cycle of drama, sensationalism, blaming, shaming, judging, and victimization? We have to if we want to stop this runaway train. We can start seeing ourselves and each other for who we truly are, and not the persona we create to make ourselves accepted or protect our reputation. The fact is, most people find it hard to accept that it isn't necessary for *everyone* to agree with us. If others don't feel the same way you do, or fail to see the world through your eyes, that doesn't invalidate your perspective. It simply means we all have different experiences that lead to different opinions and interpretations. We need to understand that there is beauty and goodness within each of us and that we are the ones that can break the cycles of oppression and hate—not by replacing one leader or regime with another, but through trust, relationships, and community.

Once we understand that we can learn from the past—that it can give us the strength and courage to trek into the unknown with a deep desire to heal—we can truly let go of the chains that keep us stuck in a story that needs to end so a healthy one can emerge. I have let go of so many stories and people during this lifetime, as I get up every morning and experiment with possibilities and do my own inner work. It's the hardest work I have ever done, and I would do it again, as it is also the most rewarding. It has been scary at times, as I took my wobbly steps into the unknown, but over time I've taught myself, with the help of nature and the universe, to embrace the challenges as opportunities.

Many people think things are simply happening *to* us, and we fall into the trap of being a victim over and over again. I learned that it was my choice whether I wanted to live in a world of blame and victimization. I could stand in line, waiting for the roller coaster ride, and climb on board every hour for days. Every ride will be the same; the more we take it, the more we learn to anticipate the scary and exhilarating bits.

Our intuition simply points the way. We are blessed with powerful imaginations and equally powerful intuitions. It would be wise to follow where our inner visions might point. If you need an answer and can't seem to separate your thoughts from your feelings, watch for little signs that appear in your daily life. It could be something that catches your eye, a snippet of a conversation you overhear, or a number you keep seeing, like 11:11. There are signs and synchronicities all around us when we're ready to let them in. It might be time to step into the light and focus on the future rather than on the past. What do you want to do? Where do you want to go? What's your bigger purpose? These are healthy questions to contemplate, and the answers can likely be found in whatever you feel passionate about.

Perhaps something we can act on is aligning our values for a healthier life—sharing our talents, helping out where we can, or listening with an open heart. It seems that the universe is calling us to be movers or shakers—creating a healthy life for ourselves so we can then start creating something meaningful or impactful, something to rattle some cages by being who we are at the core, or simply by living fully within our power. Can you acknowledge whatever keeps prodding you and heed the call?

When is it time to release something that has run its course? If you've been carrying emotional baggage, perhaps *now* is the time to commit to tossing it. Or perhaps you can release yourself from a difficult situation. Either way, I invite you to experience a simpler, more spacious life, and to question whether you need as much as you think you do. The more space you create around you, the more space you create within you. Consider what you can let go of and whether you would enjoy the sense of space and peace that brings. How can you know what you're capable of if you don't embrace the unknown?

EXPEDITION 17

TREKKING INTO THE UNKNOWN

We're all having to learn—faster than we ever imagined—to get used to uncertainty and unpredictability. We might even discover there are gifts in finding comfort in not knowing what's ahead of us and living in ambiguity. Russian novelist, Fyodor Dostoevsky, once wrote, "Times of crisis, of disruption or constructive change, are not only predictable, but desirable. They mean growth. Taking a new step, uttering a new word, is what people fear most."

We can learn to forgive ourselves for past decisions and decide whether we want to hang on to them. We can attend hundreds of summits on purpose and leadership and post hundreds of tweets, but unless we experiment with life itself, they are only words. Life is not lived by following someone outside ourselves, but through action and learning how to follow our own lead instead.

AS ABOVE, SO BELOW; AS BELOW, SO ABOVE

It's time to move away from what cannot and will not change. It's time to find the courage to get to know ourselves well enough to adopt a healthy mindset, which we can use to build a new, healthy life. Now is the time to begin healing ourselves and our beautiful planet that was made for living fully. If you've made it this far, ask yourself whether you're being called to remember that you are part of nature, and check to see if you are on high alert for any signs of unnatural separation and division from yourself and others. It is your time to heal, to mend yourself with the togetherness that integrity and compassion bring into your life. When we align to natural cycles, there is no need for winning or losing—there is only movement and flow.

There's no integrity or compassion with a conflicted outlook on life. Healing our conflicts as to what is healthy or unhealthy takes a great deal of soul searching and honesty with ourselves. While our egos may punish us for being wrong or doing something "stupid," there are only consequences for our actions and inactions at any moment. We have a choice in everything that is a part of our lives, including our life experiences and what we've been taught about life, from the time we were old enough to be educated by our families and schooling. The world around you may have determined whether you were a popular kid at school or unpopular, but as you grew up, it was up to you to choose how you developed your identity, how you responded, and what you chose to believe—and whether being popular holds any significance to you at all.

We each have the capacity to choose how we allow anyone to treat us, what we believe and don't believe, what we tolerate or don't, and whether we're ready to listen to our internal compass and flow with life rather than show up every day to fight it with everything we have. We are being invited to observe and know ourselves: what food, people, and beliefs are we consuming, how are we spending our time, what are we thinking about, and what we're experimenting with.

This is an opportunity to sift through unhealed relationships with ourselves and those around us, what we have not done but have longed to do, what our calling and purpose is and why we may have not answered it, and all the ways fear blocks us from living in our power. A dear friend shared that, when he was young, his dream was to be an artist by creating custom furniture for people through his carpentry. But he found that to make it in the world and support his family, he had to design what his clients wanted most and put his dream on hold—like so many of us have when faced with the reality of providing for ourselves and a family. And now, years later in his late 50s, he's confessed that he feels too old to change anything.

Many of us face these choices, but we'll never know what the world could offer us until we follow our hearts. Like my friend, I too, silenced my childhood dream of being a writer. Instead, I took what was an "honorable" path to becoming a successful business executive until I saw that my own heart was breaking by taking a course that never truly spoke to me. I was very good at my job and kept being recognized for my hard work—but, on the inside, I was dying each day within my own conflicted world of conformity and uniformity that never spoke to my soul.

This world professes that it's more honorable for us to place making a living the priority before making life about experimentation and adventure. It has been the way of life that we constructed and agreed to through what is valued and accepted in our society. No one aspires to be a poor, starving artist or stay in a loveless marriage because it's the right thing for the kids. I personally want to live in a world where we can choose who and what we love, rather than a world where we die never allowing ourselves to fully feel alive.

Do you choose to suffer through your life and hold yourself back from the things you desire most? Or do you wish to embrace who you are? This is the intersection where many of us find ourselves, to varying degrees. We hold the responsibility, at any age, to question who we are and what we've identified through our choices and conditioning. Within the questions lie our answers. It's an opportunity not to judge or blame, but to truly become aware so we can heal, cleanse, release, imagine, and create. When we have the courage to question, we become aware that each question is an opportunity to trek into the unknown—and in that opportunity lies the mystery of who we truly are and what we want to create in our world.

When we can learn to support ourselves, we learn to support each other and the planet. Our bodies, minds, and spirits require that we pause, rest, and replenish. Let fear move over and through us, as a wave would move through the ocean or a breeze would travel through the air. There's nothing to attach to, but to learn to be still, be patient, flow, and trust the currents. Life will not be as it has been, and it's healthy to trust that inner knowing and to begin to feel a type of peace and joy within ourselves. Does that mean we no longer face challenges? Does it mean there are no roadblocks? Does it mean we're totally fulfilled in every area of our life? No, it doesn't mean that at all.

Mastery is a wonderful practice, as is transformation. However, in learning mastery, we have to overcome countless obstacles and hardships on our paths. And sometimes, everything seems harder than usual. We may feel as if we're climbing and can see a peak, yet we never seem to reach anything. The journey seems endless, and we just want to throw in the towel. And maybe we should?

When we trek into the unknown, we ultimately learn humility and patience. When the journey feels impossible, it introduces feelings in us to give up. Becoming aware of when a thought goes through your mind, or a feeling goes through your body, helps to understand that you don't need to add more energy to it. How we react matters.

We can feel whatever is going on within us, and it's much healthier to acknowledge those feelings than it is to suppress them—or worse, to allow ourselves to buy into the fear-based beliefs that fan our fears.

Human beings don't change easily. We all have parts of ourselves that resist change and want to hold on to how things have been. We get a sense of security from holding on to the past. We know it well—it feels familiar—and we hang tightly to that familiarity with the illusion that it continues to make us feel safe. But this world, as we know it, is coming apart at the seams and is fraying. Old ways of living and working are no longer viable, and, as they collapse, healthier, more evolved ways of being are birthed. This will happen as more of us question why things are being done as they have been. Then, we can examine the answers and see which ones truly resonate. When we ourselves are aligned with what we think, do, say, and are, we understand that we have choices. How will we respond to someone who is attacking us? Will we fight back, be offended, blame, judge, or simply walk away? We can set a course for our spot to surf the ocean, navigating our lives in our chosen direction.

Along the way, we might encounter beautiful islands with turtles and orcas, reefs with breathtaking wildlife, and shores with fascinating people. Will there be storms along the way? Yes, of course we will face bumps along the path, but with clarity of purpose as our guide, we'll respond with higher levels of awareness. Should we feel that we would like to change course along the way, we may do so. This is all in the evolutionary adventure of life, and how we engage matters.

We need to remember to laugh and smile often, when we can, and focus on whatever elements of joy we have in our lives. It also helps to remember that wherever we put our focus is what is likely to happen. If we focus on financial ruin, for example, and imagine ourselves having to apply for loans and benefits, these scenarios are most likely to happen. Instead, we can focus on our opportunities and challenges, and consider what it would take to live our *enough* and only take what we need.

We stand at the crossroads, deciding which path to take. We can take the old path that can keep us locked in a world of blame, pain, fear, division, and suffering. Or we can choose the unknown. All we can do is purge and make space to imagine and have a vision of what a healthy life looks like for us. There is a great deal of confusion, chaos, and conflict and it's challenging to know what's real and fake. But the smoke and mirrors are starting to be revealed, and while it's unsettling, when we can see more clearly, we can become a bit more decisive about what we're willing to step into. We may need to let go of something, return to an issue that isn't fully resolved, or embrace a new beginning.

As I faced my own crossroad, I learned not to be enticed by shiny objects or credentialed famous people providing false promises. Being grounded in reality meant seeing through the illusions and delusions of the world I was a part of and learning how to ground myself in reality. I couldn't snap my fingers and manifest my mortgage payment just by visualizing it and thinking positively. In one of my failed partnerships, I was told over and over that "I can manifest anything just by thinking about it" and to simply observe Keith for his amazing ability to manifest whatever he desires. And as we spent a great deal of time together, I experienced Keith as an incredibly exhausted man who may have been manifesting many successes while attempting to fix the world—but he was also suppressing the brokenness inside of him. And I was reminded, once again, that true freedom is experienced from unleashing our full potential and going deep into the corners of our mind so we can free it from the known. I continued learning a universal lesson: *don't let anyone tell you who you are.* "As above, so below, as within, so without, as the universe, so the soul . . . " whispers Hermes Trismegistus.

ARE YOU READY TO PUT DOWN THE MANUAL OF SUCCESS AND TREK INTO THE UNKNOWN?

There is an inner awareness that we were conditioned and trained to silence within ourselves when we were handed the universal manual of success. It included deep programming of what's considered good and what's bad, and it was constructed for the lowest common denominator.

It takes a village caring for each other to truly make a difference. Choosing unity, connection, and creation is a conscious choice. Many have forgotten what this means in pursuit of never-ending programming of success and fear, which need constant feeding and depletes most souls. It's the current model of service to self where we focus solely on our own survival.

We can choose to claim our power and use it wisely. We've been taught that we're powerless. We've been taught that the world is out of our control. We've learned that someone outside ourselves gives us power and validation. And yet, we can choose to address any limiting beliefs and societal conditioning that hold us back in any way. When we're no longer held back, it's entirely up to us to step into our true power. Let's learn to celebrate being in our power through the choices we make—like how we spend our time here on Earth, and the mindset we empower ourselves to have. In *F*ck the Bucket List for the Health Conscious: Trusting Your Heart,* we explore that one of the healthiest things we can do for ourselves is relearning to trust our internal navigation system— our intuition. The external noise will grow, regardless. But what's your gut whispering to you when you put down the manual you were given?

HAVE YOU EVER PLANTED SEEDS IN A GARDEN?

If you have ever started a garden, did you dig deep in the soil and create a deep well? Did you dig your hands deeper and deeper in the earth until the seeds found their healthy home?

When you plant something new, you heave up the earth. Then, once the seeds are planted in the ground, you smooth out the soil, add water, and wait for the intelligence of nature to take flight. You may pick the weeds when they appear, and make sure your plant doesn't have any parasites hanging on to its roots. It is also entirely possible that your seed will simply die and never transform from a plant to a squash.

There's growing unrest in the world. It has always been here. The difference is that there are people questioning and becoming more aware that we created borders, countries, wars, divisions, propaganda, and laws. Instead of being outraged and manipulated, what can we do? What happens when we tap into our power—not with more anger and fear, but rather with an understanding that we don't need more talk around the problems we created and instead need to imagine and create healthier systems? We need to question why we built the foundation we're standing on and whether it supports us—and if not, what can we do? We can criticize our failing education system and rage against it, or we can use our brilliant minds and hearts to create something better for our children and the next generations.

There's growing awareness that wars do not happen on their own; they are created by those supporting division and drawing battle lines in the sand. You no longer need to accept the status quo or generic answers that don't resonate with you. Over the next few years, antiquated patterns that have been accepted—such as, "this is just the way things are done here"—will be called into question as we dig deeper and deeper into our very being.

More and more people are starting to plant healthy seeds in individual and collective gardens. But to do so, we're digging deep in the dirt and weeding out the toxicity—be it beliefs, people, or food. Spending time in nature increases our awareness that everything is alive—until it's not. Natural cycles teach us everything there is to know about life and death. The tree in a garden will witness more people in its lifetime than a human ever will.

Trekking into the unknown is a message of hope. When we worry about what's going on in the world and fear for our future, we can find solace in the natural world, where so much is invisible to us. The waves we're riding are bumpy and are characterized by highs and lows. When we hit a low, we might question whether the wave will come crashing down on us and sweep us away. But we cannot expect life, or any human, to never encounter turbulence. Life is in flow, like the ocean. One wave might crash down on us and the next might take us onto unknown heights.

We have been conditioned to do what's expected of us. People will tell us, "I know what's best for you," or "I know what you need to do." We may have ended up trusting someone and opening ourselves to the hurt of disappointment. When we think back to that situation, the memory can spark a certain fear and shame in us. But while it may feel very real, it's just a memory. It doesn't need to paralyze us.

Many people spend much of their lives caged by a memory of where they've been or what they've experienced and keep playing the same movie and its sequel over in our mind. When we realize that we're still alive, and that experience was there to teach us something, we can let the memory go. Some people are like a raging thunderstorm, while others are more like calming waterfalls. We get to choose who we surround ourselves with.

Keep breathing. Our mindset matters. Life is unpredictable, as is nature. One day there is calm, and the next, an unexpected storm can come from around the bend and surprise us. After some time, the storm will pass. Some will last a few days, while others will be shorter. These storms will not only take place outdoors, they will come in the form of people inviting us to be part of their outrage at whatever controversy is playing out on their screens. We don't have to be swept away in a storm of anger and fear. These storms will pass, and we don't need to engage with what does not resonate with us. We can simply keep breathing and choose to smile, laugh, or cry.

On a scale from 1 to 10, where 1 is not at all and 10 is always, how much would you say you are able to be your true self in an average day? Are you doing what you want to do when you want to do it—or are you confined, restricted, or somehow unable to express your true self? Let your answers guide you.

Our own navigation system—the body, heart, and spirit—will tell us what it needs at every moment, provided we are tuned into ourselves. Some of us push ourselves to go to the gym to live up to a goal, while all our body wants is rest. It's important to move and be active and be conscious of consuming natural food—but to live fully, we can make space to trek into possibilities and the unknown.

Flow doesn't come with resistance. Resistance often shows up as disease and illness that generates stress. Many of the diseases and illnesses we experience come from pushing against the flow of allowing ourselves to simply *be*. There is healthy stress that challenges our boundaries and comfort zones. It asks us to discern between doing and being.

By simply getting this far into this series, you are being called to trek into the unknown, which provides abundant possibilities and opportunities to be who you came here to be. It's about being curious about what's around the bend and exploring with a desire to live a healthy life on this planet. It's about becoming aware that our opportunity is to create what we need most by constructing healthy foundations and systems, as well as trusted relationships and communities that lift us up and serve us. Healthy relationships can be formed, while destructive unions can be left behind. We get to practice until we reach our own mastery. And we will arrive when there will be no need for books like this to activate us and light our way.

Doors and paths are now opening to a more mysterious and spiritual way of living. It's in your hands. All you have to do is step through them or on them. When you want your life to change, you must be the one who makes it happen. You have more creative power than you realize, and now is the time to see yourself as the architect of your life. Whatever your passion is—whatever your unique way of connecting, serving, or creating may be—*now* is the time to find it and make a difference. Be brave, be bold, and trust yourself like never before. Aldous Huxley joins us with this insight: "For every traveler who has any taste of his own, the only useful guidebook will be the one which he himself has written." If there is one actionable thing you could do that would help you become aware of what's calling you, what would it be?

EXPEDITION 18

INITIATION INTO THE UNKNOWN: NOW WHAT?

One of the many questions to explore as you venture into the unknown is who holds your power. When you keep fighting for everything, you acknowledge someone else holds the key to your life. When you argue in a never-ending need to win and be right, you miss the opportunity to engage in a healthy dialogue that connects you to new possibilities—especially within yourself. Why have we been conditioned to trust others before fully trusting ourselves? Why do so many simply want to be seen, validated, and recognized as winners and superheroes? In the end, who wins what?

More division is simply a neat separation into labels and categories, which usually infuses a need to fight for our lives for our very survival. When we keep taking sides as warriors in a battle or conflict, we're not creating—we are simply stuck fighting within the walls of an existing paradigm or system where we know exactly what happens to the winners and the losers, and where the oppressed most likely become the oppressors.

Mystic philosopher, Sri Aurobindo, has said, "Watch the too indignantly righteous. Before long you will find them committing or condoning the very offense which they have so fiercely censured." This is not only our current reality, but the television shows and films we invite into our lives as entertainment. We replay these stories over and over, seeking the justice and freedom we hold inside ourselves, waiting for permission to be free by some invisible authority figure who holds power over us.

It has been honorable to fight and be right until this point in our own history. But instead of correcting the injustices of our past, our future is calling us to create healthy foundations that don't always require us to battle throughout our time here. We need to apply our abundant human intelligence to discern between what is working and what is dying within us. In her life-changing book, *Little Fires Everywhere*, Celeste Ng shares, "Sometimes you need to scorch everything to the ground and start over. After the burning, the soil is richer, and new things can grow. People are like that, too. They start over. They find a way."

When we're stuck in a maze, we're in a structure looking for the way out. We may be facing two options, two sides, two choices within the maze—but what if there were additional options that we can't even imagine or see? How could we when everything around us has already been set in stone? Paulo Coelho reminds us that, "I can choose either to be a victim of the world or an adventurer in search of treasure. It's all a question of how I view my life."

There's a great deal of unlearning for each of us to discover for ourselves. No one can do this work for us. It's about accepting responsibility and facing ourselves. We can't continue the cycles of blame. Whatever got us here doesn't need to be a force of self-destruction or stagnation in life. While terrible things may have happened to us, we can transform them into an opportunity to break cycles. But when we take no responsibility and blame the government, our parents, our partner, or even our ancestors for everything, we have given up on the future.

There's another way. There are many heart-centered people who can help us, but the first step is to have a desire to be the architect of our own precious life. It's up to you and the choices you make in this moment. Many of us are realizing that things are not always as they seem, and those who are fearful of trekking into the unknown try to shame and silence us for doing so. Can you imagine living in a world with powerful, conscious architects and creators who, instead of dissecting the past (with endless breaking news and expert commentary), are transforming problems into our greatest opportunities to live in balance with nature, ourselves, and each other? What is purpose if not our ability to imagine and create with deep meaning? Imagine living in a world where our structures and systems support us, rather than divide us. What can you envision? There is hope when we choose to let go.

"'How does one become a butterfly?' she asked pensively.

"'You must want to fly so much that you are willing to give up being a caterpillar.'

"'You mean to die?' asked Yellow, remembering the three who fell out of the sky.

"'Yes and no,' he answered.

"'What looks like you will die, but what's really you will still live.'"

— Trina Paulus, *Hope for the Flowers*

TRUSTING THE CURRENTS

Rivers remain unattached to all that goes through them and around them. Leaves and sticks loosen along the banks and bottoms of the river and get swept away by the currents. Rivers flow and welcome all they come across. And they also let go. They understand that the water is a form of cleansing and refreshing their operating system.

But what about us? Can we learn to let go of our attachments to the stories of how life was supposed to play out with its dramas, people, beliefs, and past experiences that keep us imprisoned and fighting for our liberation? Can we release what isn't ours, like the baggage we've been hanging on to? The conflicts, envy, fears, limiting beliefs, unhealthy people, and the practice of belittling, blaming, and judging ourselves and others? Is life a problem to be fixed or an opportunity to face the unknown by relinquishing the painful stories of the past and mistakes we've made along the way? Allowing everything to surge through us, like the river, allows us to purge and cleanse with mindfulness and curiosity for what's possible. And like nature teaches us, there is no need to rush, as we can also let go of the attachment to achievement and winning.

Now, imagine that you're having a conversation with the river. It invites you to experience its life force by jumping into its water. As you feel the current, you hesitate and wonder if this is the smartest or dumbest thing you've ever done. But there is no going back. Are you feeling fear permeate through your bones? Are you curious and flowing with the water, or do you wish you could be back on land? Are you laughing from deep inside your belly and experiencing pure joy, or are you yelling at the top of your lungs, trying to hang on? Are you entranced by the sound of the water, the leaves joining you as you pass them on the banks, and the frogs cheering you on?

We're provided with ample opportunities to let go or walk away from unhealthy situations and people throughout our lives. On the journey of self-awareness, we're called to get in touch with our courage and activate ourselves. Life is asking us to create a relationship with the unknown and engage with the mystery of it all.

The unknown brings out the adventurer in us. While it can be scary to enter the unknown, when we are able to acknowledge our fears, we can start freeing ourselves. But it can be much more frightening to allow our fears to rule us forever. By joining the river, even in our imagination, we're embarking on a vast sea of wonder and possibility in the unknown—and yet, learning to slowly trust the currents that we will face each step of the way.

When we stop needing to prove to ourselves and others that we're worthy, we accept the essence of who we are. There's no need to spend our lives trying to change the world and be accepted into it. The more we focus on what we know, the more energy we give to the status quo. There is a vast difference between trying to change the rules and realizing there is no rule book to change. The pioneers set off into the unknown, and they are rarely celebrated as we set out on our own adventures. But it's never been about being liked or popular; that's just a defense mechanism for holding our power.

Instead of spending our lives trying to prove ourselves to anyone else, we set out on our own path. The same type of people and situations will appear, maybe with a different name, head and body, until we break our patterns and allow our energies to align and flow by being grounded. This is where my freedom begins. I want to live a quiet life by a swimmable ocean and help open hearts and minds to possibilities without fighting or creating a following. My mission is to offer medicine for the soul. I imagine millions and millions of people in every corner of the world who can take what they need from these books, and experience life to the fullest as powerful co-creators. It's about you and me bringing meaning to our lives by taking action.

The joy comes from sparking conversations and expeditions for anyone who's ready to step into the emerging world of possibilities. Where do you begin to take impeccable care of yourself? What's your initiation to the unknown?

THINGS THAT INSPIRE

We've often believed that work is a place we go to make a living or a way to define who we are in the world. The first question we ask or are asked is, "What do you do? Where are you from? Where did you grow up?" These questions make it clear what box or label we belong to and to filter who we connect with based on the labels we were given. We rarely hear someone say (and I hope this changes soon), "I was born to be a dad to three boys, each who are my most cherished gifts, and I do everything to help them see there's a healthy way to live. I teach them that life is not easy work, and that my boy who was born with autism shines a bright light on our world. I want them to create a balanced life where they don't need to mask or flee grief, pain, or sadness to find joy. I am raising children with my partner with deep meaning, compassion, and love to create the world we all deserve to live in." Now, imagine the unknown meaning of compassion being our ability to give and receive equally, and that harm to self or another was impossible. What questions would we be asking to truly connect with ourselves and one another?

In *The Velveteen Rabbit*, Margery Williams tells us, "It doesn't happen all at once . . . You become. It takes a long time. That's why it doesn't happen often to people who break easily, or have sharp edges, or who have to be carefully kept. Generally, by the time you are Real, most of your hair has been loved off, and your eyes drop out and you get loose in the joints and very shabby. But these things don't matter at all, because once you are Real you can't be ugly, except to people who don't understand."

We can each have meaningful conversations with ourselves and get comfortable with the silence, too. And if someone wants to fight, that's his or her right—but never at our own expense. We can choose forgiveness, kindness, and curiosity. The following are some of the essential messages of my initiation into the unknown—it's up to you to create your own.

One of the first things I realized was that *no one knows anything for sure*, regardless of the titles, certificates, and expertise they hold, especially when it comes to living my life. Sure, they have opinions and can offer advice. But it's up to me to make decisions as to how I want to spend my time on Earth. Just like a glass shattering, it's up to me to pick up the broken pieces and deal with my own pain while learning not to drag the shards along with me wherever I go. When we're healthy, there's something raw and real about experiencing life.

This brings me to the second breakthrough I had, which was to tap into my younger self and remember that *our imagination provides us the courage to experiment and create.* Growing from life's challenges, and what I felt were unjust setbacks, has helped me shake off an attitude of victimhood and carve a more determined course toward my life's fulfillment. Imagination and humor are potent tools to get us through the rough times and break free. I started imagining the door opening for me to take a big step forward in life. I was prepared to take some bold steps toward changing restrictions in my life and opening up to a broader range of imagination and the courage to evolve. I learned to let go of limiting beliefs, destructive relationships, and anything else that kept me from taking steps into the unknown.

It also greatly helped when I started to *question everything*. I started to experience firsthand that things were not as I was taught and conditioned to believe. I felt blessed to live in a time where abundant information was available to me (which was sometimes overwhelming), and I encountered people and resources I would never have come across otherwise. I found that I can reach out to people and have conversations that I never imagined. To do so, I had to also slow down, go within, and ask deeper questions. It made me understand that we're not here to solve problems, but to see the opportunities in everything—and to do so, we must get to the root cause and source of everything. When I faced a problem, I started questioning what the opportunity was, and what was within my power to create. I looked at what was working (healthy) and what wasn't (toxic) as the framework and guidance in breaking patterns and experiencing more joy.

There were days, weeks, and months I spent alone, reflecting and writing at all hours of the day. I *examined the foundation* of my world and came to a healthier level of awareness and plane of reality. When I studied our separation from nature and our constant need to survive and win at all costs, it was heartbreaking to take it all in. But I kept at it. Every once in a while, I would step into old patterns, feeling the weight of the world on my shoulders and realizing how much I don't belong to the stories of the past any longer. Once I understood that life is to be experienced and there is no destination, no ladder to climb, no award to receive, no reason to be better than anyone else, I could simply *be*.

What I learned was that it was really up to no one else but me to get through the uncertain times and make the most of the opportunity for a reset, knowing that life would never be the same. It couldn't. It was time to let go of everything—and every attachment that was toxic. Something always has to die to make room for what's about to be born. Sometimes we have to lose our mind and allow ourselves to break open. There's something about stripping away our old identity with all we've been carrying in our baggage, whether material items or beliefs. It was time to trek into the unknown with wonder and awe, *no longer giving a fuck about what anyone else thought was best for me.*

THERE'S ALWAYS A HEALTHY
PATH WHEN WE'RE WHOLE

Have you—or someone you witnessed—ever thrown a temper tantrum, stamping your feet, flailing your arms, crying out against the injustice of it all? Have you been told that what doesn't kill you, makes you stronger? We're taught to dream and set goals, to continuously aspire for greatness. We've been trained to get our way—and we get used to having what we want, when we want it. That's why we stamp our feet when we feel unsafe or outraged, and when things don't go our way. And we may freak out when everything that used to represent normalcy suddenly gets swept aside and becomes uncertain.

It's like we entered a void of uncertainty where we don't know what could happen. I know firsthand how confusing it can be to see the world as it is and acknowledge no longer fitting in. I knew I couldn't go back on the same route, but I also paused to feel everything deeply. It's easy to get stuck and go down a rabbit hole when we encounter only darkness in the world. When we watch a storm, the wind comes from different directions, and the heat from the water rises, and every element affects the direction and speed of the storm. Storms sometimes come into our lives to teach us and make us stronger. No one is 100 percent immune from a storm coming his or her way. The key is not to dwell on it to the point that we get stuck in the eye of the storm, but to anticipate the ebb and flow of life.

This is why pausing is an important skill to have—but it's far from easy. We spend much of our lives being influenced by other people's expectations of us, from parents to friends and even employers. We get so busy with living up to our expectations that solitude often escapes us. But a beneficial aspect of being with ourselves is figuring out who we want to actually be. Whole new fields of possibility open up to us.

It's time to see and act holistically and with unity, not conformity or uniformity. Everything in the universe is connected by design. Remember that, when we're all sad and fearful, this energy storms and vibrates through all of us. Many storms appear in our lives and our world. There's strength in uncovering pure joy and rewiring our energy source to have more balance. Every person who is ready to journey into the unknown is being asked to face his or her fears and limiting beliefs. Allow yourself to emerge with a vision and understanding of why you are here. What do you want to build and create? And don't forget to sing, dance, run, scream, let go, cleanse, so you can create what's in your heart through alchemy and pure authentic love of yourself and the planet.

In this current reality, no one's path is easy. But when you stop comparing yoursef and living up to the expectations, you'll find yourself alone—discovering the courage to leave the harbor and trust the current. And maybe, like me, you'll also find a deep gratitude for everything—the terrifying places the mind takes you, the failures, the heartbreaks, and the breakthroughs. Taking steps into the unknown and inviting healthy experiences expand your horizons. When you're no longer a victim of your situation and systems, you choose discomfort and uncertainty with an open heart. British poet, Alfred Tennyson, reminds us, "The shell must break before the bird can fly." Please love yourself enough to take your own leap of faith and soar into your unknown.

When one stage of our journey ends, another begins. See you soon in our continuing journey in, *F*ck the Bucket List for the Health Conscious: Trusting Your Heart.*

NEVER LIE TO YOURSELF

EPILOGUE

EPILOGUE

n a noisy world—within yourself and outside yourself—it's easy to fall out of balance. It can be challenging to get a hold of yourself when you feel everything is changing quickly or falling apart. And yes, things do fall apart. It's natural to get a bit lost when everything is out of whack. What many of us are witnessing is fear and anger spilling out everywhere, and our individual and collective inability to accept what we now truly see when we question everything in healthy ways—which is actually possible when we choose to trek into the unknown.

What if, instead of seeking perfection, we understood that we're here to experience our gift of being human with all of its quirks? What if we bring more play into our lives and take ourselves less seriously? It doesn't mean we're less responsible and accountable—it means we let go of unhealthy beliefs that keep us chained to stuff that makes no sense. It means freeing ourselves from what crushes the human spirit. Taking a world of war, human trafficking, inequality, and so many atrocities off life support by stepping into our power to make healthy choices and live meaningful lives of unity. What if we get to co-create with nature and respect its abundant gifts, ourselves, and each other?

Understand that things can and will get out of control in a world where we've been taught to fight for our lives. We can choose to believe it's a game of survival of the fittest, or not. But we don't have to carry the burdens of this world on our backs every day.

When we take a cleansing breath and sit within our own calling, no matter how big or small, we tap into our own power to decide which path is calling us. And as we see more and more paths to choose from, we can take the first steps and remember we are on a journey of creation.

As humans, we can take as many "wrong" turns as we need and also recalibrate until we stand in balance and wholeness by claiming our path and trusting it. This is part of our experience, which can be challenging for us to understand as we integrate and stop censoring ourselves. Trekking into the unknown, and standing within who we truly are, is new for all of us. Much changes when we realize there's no destination to arrive at and no medal to adorn—only life to experience when we learn to trust our hearts. You were born for these times to discover what is calling you to find the courage to weave a fulfilling adventure.

There are a lot of amazing things happening in our world that you can choose to be a part of when you awaken to your power. There is an increasing number of organic farmers tending the Earth and growing non-toxic food that fuels us. There are amazing practitioners offering bodywork, energy work, and sound healing to help us become whole. There are people and communities coming together with pure intention and clarity of purpose to co-create what is needed most. There are heart-centered technologists and innovators creating open-source platforms for our time. There are teachers and educators creating alternative ways of learning that introduce ways to bring more dialogue and connection to our children. There are conscious leaders writing new stories about what works means and offering healthy workplaces for people to bring our talents and practice our craft. Many are architecting systems that are in alignment with the needs of people, communities and the planet. All this can be a rich cycle in which to develop imaginative and ingenious alternative innovations and methods of unlocking the limitations imposed on your life.

Authors Margaret Wheatley and Deborah Frieze know firsthand that it's not easy to be ahead of the curve: "Pioneers have to expect to feel ignored, invisible and lonely a good portion of the time. What they're doing is so new and different that others can't see their work even when it's staring them in the face. These are difficult dynamics to live with, especially when you know you've done good work, that you've solved problems that others are still struggling with. This is why it's so important that pioneers work as community, encouraging one another through the trials and risks natural to those giving birth to the new in the midst of the breakdown of the old."

You have access to tools—both within you and around you—that you would not have considered in the past. So, the question now becomes, what do you choose to create? And who will you create with?

You were born for this time in history. You matter and we need you to step into your power when you are ready. All our lives depend on the courage of pioneers like you, in every corner of the world, to trek into the unknown with an open heart and the mindset of an adventurer.

THE MISSION OF F*CK
THE BUCKET LIST

I hope you've been sparked and ignited to become more aware of how you want to paint your story. Is it your time to open up healthy paths of fulfillment as you head to your future? When you choose to be an architect and an adventurer, it's about taking the road less traveled by reimagining what is possible. When you choose to pause and do your work, please consider the following:

(BOOK 1)
DISCOVER THE WONDER OF YOU

Each one of us is unique and has treasures deep within us. Our presence impacts those around us, often in ways that are unspoken. When a cup is empty, it's impossible to fill another—and when a sponge is filled with water, it cannot absorb anything else. The key is to learn to take impeccable care of yourself and to trust your intuition to guide you to what's needed. Never give up but do learn to let go of unhealthy people and situations. Allow the beauty within to find its expression and let your inner beauty shine.

Your responsibility is to listen to what is calling you through deep self-awareness, and for each of us to add our value to humanity in our own unique way. How you choose to live your life is the bottom line. You can sit and watch life pass you by, crossing items off the list, or you can jump in and become a healthy creator of your own life. It's a choice.

This adventure called life is filled with the potential to create your own map and navigation system. The hardest work you'll ever be called to do is not at a job or on someone else's payroll, it's when you awaken to your voice and act on the treasures you uncover within. You are the main act of your life, and it's up to you to unleash your imagination to create opportunities.

(BOOK 2)
TREK INTO THE UNKNOWN AS AN ADVENTURER

There comes a time when it's important to close the door on the past in order to trek into the unknown. It's always helpful to be aware of the need to let go and make space for possibilities. It could be something we no longer need or use, or it could be baggage we've been carrying around for way too long. When something painful or unpleasant comes up, then it may be time to release it.

As we do, we'll feel lighter and more energized. We might also consider all that we're learning about ourselves, so we put it into action. This is a time when we can enjoy our harvest, but it's important not to be weighed down by the past and stories that no longer serve us. I often had to change direction and, on some occasions, lost my way. Despite everything, though, it was only when I paused that I began to see I was not lost at all—at least in the traditional sense. I also realized that "never burn your bridges" was a limiting belief holding me back. I simply learned which bridges should be crossed and which should be burned.

Trekking into the unknown gives us permission to experiment with being a free spirit by not being stuck in someone else's story. Our life no longer depends on anyone else's survival, because we're more powerful than we could have ever imagined when we know our hearts and minds. We're deeply connected to nature as a curious and courageous adventurer—a dreamer, an architect, and a creator of a healthy life. We know there's only one success: living our lives in our own ways. Our self-love shines on the life and communities we build, and we know a healthy world is possible.

(BOOK 3)
TRUSTING YOUR HEART AND BEING HEALTH CONSCIOUS

Once we realize there's always a way—whether we like it or not—so much can shift. Artist and spiritual teacher, Florence Scovel Shinn, once said, "Intuition is a spiritual faculty and does not explain, but simply points the way." When we're not sure of the way forward or the answer to a particular question, the path lies in being still and hearing our inner voices. This can be felt as an inner knowing or a feeling—or we might have a profound dream or a sign from the Universe. These are all valid ways of tuning in to the wise part of us that is all-knowing, so we have no need to feel powerless. We might have to alter our definition of power from being in charge to surrendering and trusting the currents.

In *The Little Prince*, Antoine de Saint-Exupéry reminds us, "It is only with the heart that one can see rightly; what is essential is invisible to the eye." Simply learn to listen to your gut. Feel free to ask it questions, but also respect it by fully being in tune with what it is whispering to you. Once the whispers become clearer, you can listen to it as quietly or as loudly as you prefer. And if something is stopping you, invest the energy in understanding where fear or worry stem from so you can assess the root cause and then listen some more. Your schooling may have taught you to think logically, but your heart never lies.

TO BE CONTINUED . . .

F*ck the Bucket List for the Health-Conscious:
Trusting Your Heart

Made in the USA
Middletown, DE
09 February 2021